MATTHEW

MEGAN McKENNA

MATTHEW

THE BOOK
OF MERCY

New City Press
Hyde Park, New York

Dedicated to

Romano Stephen Almagno, O.F.M.

Lover of the Word Made Flesh,
and of all books that speak the Truth,
teacher, librarian, preacher
and simply a son and brother of Francis
the poor man, beloved of God, and friend.
With gratitude and love.

Published in the United States by New City Press
202 Cardinal Rd., Hyde Park, NY 12538
www.newcitypress.com
©2007 Megan McKenna

Cover design by Durva Correia

Scripture quotations are taken from
The New American Bible
© 2002 United States Conference
of Catholic Bishops

Library of Congress Cataloging-in-Publication Data:

McKenna, Megan.
    Matthew : the book of mercy / Megan McKenna.
      p. cm.
    Includes bibliographical references (p. 198).

    ISBN: 978-1-56548-279-1 (alk. paper)
  1. Bible. N.T. Matthew--Commentaries. I. Title.
BS2575.53.M425 2007
226.2'07--dc22
                                    2007022341

Printed in the United States of America

Contents

Introduction

Matthew is a Jew, an Israelite steeped in the law, the prophets and the living traditions of his people. And he is the writer and scribe that seeks to pass on the vital importance of Jesus' Jewishness and Jesus' fulfillment of all that has gone before in the testament, the history and the life of the people of Israel, the people of Yahweh God. There is a rabbinical story that speaks of four kinds of students that the rabbis had in their classes. I've heard it told a number of different ways but I think the original source is in the *Talmud*, Pirke Avot 5.

* Once upon a time a group of rabbis started to discuss the kinds of students they'd had in their classes or were dealing with at the time. The first rabbi said: "I have a lot of students that are like funnels. They are so hard to deal with — they don't listen or absorb anything. It seems no matter what I say it goes in one ear and out the other. Nothing stays with them." The other rabbis nodded. They knew those students too.

   Another rabbi said: "I seem to have far too many students that are like strainers. I endeavor to pour knowledge into them, and they sift it and strain it out. Unfortunately they keep all the trivial and unimportant small bits of things and lose all the essentials of meaning and perception. They are fascinated by superficial information and, worse, they think they collect these bits and they know everything! In reality they're worse off than if they hadn't studied at all. They are unaware of the richness that they have missed altogether. I sometimes feel like they take a great bottle of wine and pour it through a strainer. They celebrate the sediment and have never tasted the wine. It is so discouraging and frustrating." Again the other rabbis all nodded in agreement.

The next rabbi said: "I used to think that I loved the student that was like a sponge, and I rejoiced when it appeared that I had one of these. They sucked up everything and could hold a great deal of knowledge, but then I realized that they needed a place to absorb it, to let it seep through their lives. And often they didn't follow through on that process and they would drip their knowledge and information wherever they went. And they stayed with their initial saturation, finding it hard to go deeper and deeper into the text, the commentary, and the dialogues with those who had studied the text before them." And there were sighs this time as each remembered a student they had hoped would be a true teacher but only had moments of insight, not a lifetime of seeking understanding.

And then another rabbi said: "I think the best kind of student is like a sieve. Such students learn to pass the information, of which there is so much, through their minds and hearts, in discussions and study of the texts but they keep the best of it. It's as though they were panning for gold and quickly learn to spot the small nuggets that are pure gold. They sift and shake the material as it is done at harvest, keep the grains of wheat that will feed the body and soul, and let all the chaff and dust and dirt fall away. They get the kernel of truth, and so they know where to begin. And they know what they don't know. That sense of humility allows them to delve ever deeper into the mysteries." There was silence this time and one of the older rabbis said: "Blessed be the Holy One; I hope we are still like the student and the sieve."

The Gospel of Matthew appears first in the canon of gospels yet is written more than fifty years after the death and resurrection of Jesus and twenty-five years after the Gospel of Mark appears. It is often referred to as the gospel for in-house church, because it concentrates so heavily on the relations that are to prevail among Christians, and focuses on providing an identity for a group of people struggling to become something altogether new, after they have lost or been excluded from so much of what constituted who they saw themselves to be in the world. Matthew is a consummate theologian, spiritual, director, disciple, and scribe. For those of us who live in a world of literacy, not just of books and libraries but of computers and iPods and memory sticks, it is hard to imagine what it was like to absorb the teachings of Jesus orally, in heart and memory, gleaning from many sources and people's experiences the core of Jesus' teachings. But Matthew took to heart Jesus' words, "Take my yoke upon you and learn from me, for I am meek and humble of heart" (Mt 11:29). He also took to heart Jesus' words when confronting the teachers and rabbis concerning their experience of Judaism and weaves them through all of Jesus' teachings.

> As for you, do not be called "Rabbi." You have but one teacher, and you are all brothers. Call no one on earth your father, you have but one Father in heaven. Do not be called "Master"; you have but one master, the Messiah. The greatest among you must be your servant. Whoever exalts himself will be humbled, but whoever humbles himself will be exalted. (Mt 23:8–12)

Matthew has learned well. And so Matthew, a true student, a true disciple, becomes a master in the tradition of his Lord and Teacher, Jesus. One of Matthew's singular and foundational gifts is to pass along the knowledge of Judaism, the history of the covenant, the prophets, the law, and the long expectation that fed the people's souls over a thousand years before the coming of the Word made flesh that dwells among us now. Matthew's Jesus is Jewish and, like the good disciple and good scribe, Matthew sifts through the ancient texts, beliefs, and interpretations, culls out the best and most insightful of the old, and layers it into Jesus' fresh and dynamic insights given by the Spirit. Matthew reveals a depth and shift in knowing God our Father, retaining the basis of how we are to live in the world as believers in God. He sees how Jesus was steeped in the psalms, the prophets, the law and the covenant, and went ever deeper into it, and then extended it out further, breaking the bound-aries of one people and their particular heritage to include all the peoples of the world in God's embrace and to invite all into the communion of the kingdom of heaven on earth, and into the inti-macy of the Godhead of the Trinity, the community par excellence.

Matthew has absorbed Jesus' wisdom, and in the power of the Spirit has passed it along to all succeeding generations. He does not teach himself, only the person of Jesus. He tells the story of his own call to be a disciple in chapter 9, following Jesus' healing of a paralytic because of the devotion and faith of the man's friends. Matthew includes himself among the public sinners — they are his friends. Jesus eats with them, breaking social mores and taboos that separate people into groups of sinner and righteous, clean and unclean, worthy and unworthy. As a Jew Matthew came from that "unclean" world into the house of Jesus where mercy reigned, and in forgiveness all was put behind so that the power of God's goodness could be seen and God the Father could be glorified and given thanks.

The Word became flesh in Jesus and God became Emmanuel, God-with-us. And Matthew was one of the first to take that Word and incorporate it into his own flesh and sift it through his mind and heart, living it daily. Then he put it into words, inspired by the power of the Spirit of God so that others could hear Jesus' Word and know him inti-mately. Matthew's Gospel brings Jesus across national borders and boundaries of time, language, culture, and tradition. And Matthew brings it with the rich layers of Jewish writing and honor for the text of scripture. The Jewish schema assigns forty-four levels of meaning to every word, phrase, letter, punctuation mark, and even space or gap on a page of scripture. Words are doorways into the endless depth and meaning of the mystery written there. In the Torah, called "black fire on white fire," was hidden God's presence and power. The scripture both revealed and concealed, waiting to be uncovered, discovered, and shared. Matthew's Gospel is written in this rich tradition and must be read against this background.

Matthew's Gospel is the Book of the Scribe. Again, we are used to communicating and sharing information through typing, talking, text messaging, digital pictures, websites, and an array of electronic and technological media. Matthew wrote his Gospel in longhand on scrolls. It was work and it was a lifestyle of transmission. As Jesus sent the disciples out to make disciples from every nation, Matthew used his scrolls and pens to pass on the gospel in a form that everyone could take with them.

I am a storyteller and most of what I teach I learn orally and then transmit orally before I put it down on paper. The transition is a work of translation, an art form in itself. When I learn a story, especially when I learn a portion of the gospels by heart (different from merely memorizing it), I often write it out in longhand a number of times so that I get a feel for the words on paper before I put them into my mouth. This process coordinates something between the brain and the eye, the heart and the hand, before it starts to connect between the ear and the tongue.

I have been fascinated by words as long as I can remember, and I love to write. And oddly enough I have learned that I write in totally different ways depending on the instrument I use to write: a pencil, a pen, a fountain pen, or a computer. Things more intimately connected to the Spirit, and to communicating with people, I write out in longhand, and I prefer a fountain pen or a gel pen — it flows more smoothly. I write out my sermons, poetry, stories as I learn to tell them, and portions of the scripture. I write out my talks and classes. Then once I have given them or taught them, I can write on a computer. The stories have been incorporated into my body, mind, and heart and I have lived with them, and — I hope — lived them before they go down on the paper. And all the materials — books, sermons, talks, etc. — have been culled from many people's beliefs, experience, failures, knowledge, and wisdom.

Years ago someone gave me a poster in calligraphy titled "A Medieval Allegory of the Scribe's Tools." It comes from a medieval monastic sermon from the school of scribes at the Durham Cathedral in northern England. It interprets the tools of a scribe as spiritual aids for a Christian life. It is fascinating as history, as tradition, as a source of reflection, especially in relation to Matthew as a scribe or to anyone who teaches the scriptures:

> The *parchment* on which we write
> is pure conscience.
> The *knife* that scrapes it
> is the fear of God.
> The *pumice* that smoothes the skin
> is the discipline of heavenly desire.
> The *chalk* that whitens it
> signifies an unbroken meditation of holy thoughts.
> The *ruler* is the will of God.
> The *straight edge* is devotion to the holy task.
> The *quill* its end split in two for writing
> is the love of God and of our neighbor.
> The *ink* is humility itself.
> The *illuminator's colors*
> represent the multiform grace of heavenly wisdom.
> The *writing desk*
> is tranquility of heart.
> *The exemplar* from which a copy is made
> is the life of Christ.
> The *writing place*
> is contempt of worldly things, lifting us to a desire for
>   heaven.

The only line with which I would differ is the very last. The writing place is the experience and wonder of worldly things lifting us to a desire for heaven. With the mystery of the Incarnation, God becoming human and dwelling among us, and in the mystery of Resurrection, all the earth itself is made holy and everything and everyone groans in expectation for the coming fullness of life in Christ. So I have done a little of my own editing and calligraphy on the poster.

I have made this commentary on Matthew's Gospel with the conscious intention of helping communities incorporate this gospel into their lives together, concentrating on the underlying themes of forgiveness, reconciliation, and at-one-ment — how small communities are made, how church is held together in the world by the power of Jesus' words, the power of the Spirit, and the Fathering of

God. This was easy to do, because that is one of the main reasons that Matthew wrote his gospel. He was creating a community of Christians born of Judaism's faith and history of longing, and of Jesus' humanity and divinity in the Incarnation and Resurrection, that exploded from within every piece of revelation once given, exploding out into the world and out past the boundaries of convention and of the usual interpretations. This book is called "The Book of Mercy" because mercy is the ink, the paper, the background, the words and the meaning, in and through and under everything. Everything that Jesus says and does, his very presence and his coming upon earth, is Mercy. Jesus is the mercy of God making us beloved children, beloved brothers and sisters, beloved communities that imitate the mercy and the love within the Trinity, who are Three and yet are One. And we who are many are one in the Body of Christ through mercy. Mercy sings through the text and mercy makes sense of everything in the wisdom of God. And it is to this that we are all witnesses in the world. This is what the power of God gives us to spread and announce and exemplify with our lives. In one of his journals Thomas Merton once wrote a phrase apropos to this gospel: "mercy within mercy within mercy." It is a description of the Trinity. It is a description of what Jesus' communities, of what church is summoned to be for all peoples, but most especially for those who cry out for mercy and have never even known justice. Mercy rules. Mercy is the kingdom of heaven on earth. Mercy is what Jesus brings as good news. Mercy is Jesus' touch on every person's body. Mercy is stretched out to us in Jesus. Matthew's Gospel is a treatise on mercy.

May all of us who search the text of the scriptures and pray the Gospel of Matthew become disciples of mercy and learn to preach Mercy, live Mercy, and draw the peoples of the world into the embrace of Mercy — as we have known it and as it beckons us to come ever deeper. May we pray to be mercy on the earth as Jesus is Mercy and so be good disciples, good scribes, and good Christians. Amen.

1
The Scribe and
the Community

We begin with an old Jewish story, traditionally from Krakow, Poland. It has been called "The Dream" or "Buried Treasure," because both of these images figure strongly in the story's telling. But I have another name for it, because this particular version develops in unexpected ways from the traditional one. I hope that this story will give us some foundational insights into Matthew's Gospel, the reasons for its creation, and the audience for whom it was originally intended. And then the story can help us to read the text, as inspired for all times and peoples who believe in similar circumstances and relationships. There are many versions of the first part of the story, even a children's book called *The Treasure*, but this is how I tell it:

* Once upon a time there was a poor Jewish couple that lived in a small village. They struggled to survive, to raise their children, and to be good Jews, trusting in God's providence and being faithful. But it was hard. The land was poor. The Jews were not persecuted outright, but they were always viewed with suspicion by the government and the Christians, and there were bandits and thieves everywhere. It was so bad that the man and woman brought their one cow, their two goats, and a couple of chickens inside their one-room house so that no one would steal them during the night. This dire situation went on for

years. One morning the man woke from a dream he couldn't
wait to tell his wife. They sat at the kitchen table and he spun
out the dream; it was as real, more real, than the hard table and
chairs they sat on. He dreamed of a city, shining in the sunlight,
surrounded by water and seven bridges, and under one of the
bridges (he knew exactly where it was) there was a treasure
buried, and waiting for him! He was so excited — God, blest
be His Name, had answered their prayers.

The woman eyed him sharply and said, "Old Man, what did
you have to eat last night? All these crazy dreams! You can't
just up and go away, looking for some city of light in your
dreams! What will we do while you're gone? Put it out of your
head and get out there to work." And so he did. But he
dreamed the exact same dream the next night and told his wife
again. Again she put him off, saying, you can't go by dreams
literally, you have to know that it's just stuff inside you that is
trying to get out — and that all they thought about and prayed
about was someone or something to save them. He should go
to work. And so he did. But he dreamed the same dream again
the third night, and this time he did not tell his wife. He rose
early and scratched into the table: "Trust me. I have gone after
the treasure. I will return."

He walked all that first day and a farmer let him sleep in his
barn. He walked the next day and the next, looking for the city
over every hill. He walked for a week, working at places along
the way in exchange for something to eat and a place to sleep.
Somehow it hadn't seemed this far in his dream — just a short
distance. But he kept walking. He walked a month…. He
thought about going back, but thought of his wife, waiting for
him and the "I told you so" that he'd be met with upon his
return, and reminded of long after, and he kept walking. He
walked for three months and finally decided: it was just a
dream. He had to go back. There was one more hill — he'd
walk to the top and turn around and head for home. But when
he crested the hill, there it was! Exactly as in his dream!
Shining in the sunlight, with the water and the bridges — and
he ran for the bridge that had the treasure hidden underneath it.

But he came up short at the bridge. There was a detail he hadn't expected — a soldier guarding it. The man chatted with him, and found out that it was the same two or three guards every day. He worked in the city for a week and came out daily to share his lunch with the same soldier and to chat. Finally he decided he had to make his move. He started the conversation by saying that he'd had the strangest dream — that a treasure was buried under this very bridge. How about digging to see if it was there, and if he found anything, he'd share it with him? The soldier listened to him and laughed at him mercilessly. "What? You can't put any stock in dreams. Who knows where they come from? Why just this morning and the last couple of mornings I've been dreaming and talking to my wife." Though crestfallen the man asked him about his dream. And the soldier stunned him, saying "It's about this old shack in a small village and this couple — he looks a bit like you — who are so poor they bring their skinny cow and goats and even chickens inside the house every night so that no one will steal them. They live hand to mouth, and they don't even know that there is a treasure buried underneath their hearth stone."

The man couldn't believe his ears … he pushed the soldier for more details and he was certain — it was his own house in the soldier's dream. He excused himself as quickly as he could and ran — all the way home. It didn't take him nearly as long as the trip out. Weeks later he burst into his house, pushed the pots and stones aside and started digging, talking all the time about a treasure. His wife was both glad to see him and annoyed, and the children chatted while he dug frantically. He dug, down about four or five feet, and found nothing. Exhausted, fell into bed saying he would explain it all later. He was disappointed. He had been so sure that the dream was for him!

While he slept, the children picked up the shovel and started to imitate their father, digging in the hearth area, and soon they found a great kettle. They dragged it out and excitedly woke their father to show him their find. He wept, took the cover off, and there was his treasure! Gold coins, a number of jewels and old coins — they would never go hungry again! They would not want for anything ever again! Blest be God's Holy Name.

Being good Jews, they sorted the treasure out and put aside a portion to build a synagogue so that the villagers could have their own place of worship and not have to walk miles to pray. Then they put aside money for the widows and orphans, and for strangers passing through, so that there would always be charity and welcome for them. And then they built their house, a hen house, and a barn for their goats, sheep, and cows, and they carefully put money aside for clothes, schooling, food, necessities of life, and gifts for family, friends, and those in need. And because the soldier had shared his dream with the man, even though he laughed at him, he sent one of the jewels to him. It was only just. And their life was good and they were grateful to God, Blest be His Name.

The children went to school, grew up, married, moved away, and so it was just the man and woman again. As the years passed, they noticed that the pile of coins was dwindling, and soon there would be nothing left. They would have to start selling off some of their animals, or a piece of their land, just to eat. They had been careful stewards of the treasure, but it was running out, and by God's grace, they still would have many years left to them. They spoke about what to do. And finally they took their last coin and decided to go for a walk together, and they would find out what to do. They walked outside the town and, no sooner than they were alone, did they see a beggar coming towards them.

They looked at each other and knew — the last coin which had been the Holy One's gift to them had to go to a beggar, as their gift given. The beggar approached with outstretched hand, and they handed him their coin, smiling. The beggar looked straight into their eyes and said to them, "Dig deeper!" They looked at each other, startled, wondering what he might mean, and when they looked again, he was nowhere to be seen. They ran back to the house and once again began to dig under the hearth. Just inches down, near where they had dug before, they found a box. Upon opening it, they found Torah scrolls and a bigger treasure than the one before, with jewels. They built a study house and a place for travelers to rest and reflect on their journeys. It is said that it stood there for generations.

When these visitors awoke in the morning, they were asked about their dreams and they were invited to study the scrolls, the Word of Yahweh, and to rest a while before they would continue on their journeys. And above the door lintels were carved the words: "You must often go on a journey to find what is hidden under your own hearthstone." All this was long ago ... but what remains is the story and its wisdom for you to treasure. Remember, no matter what, Dig Deeper!

In the past when I have heard this story, it ended with the man digging under his hearth, finding the treasure, and sending a jewel off to the soldier who had laughed at him and shared his dream with him — and the notation that our dreams are for others' lives and we must communicate with others, especially enemies and strangers, to find our own sources of wisdom and wealth. Now when I tell the story, its title is "Dig Deeper" — on all levels: in the ground; for treasure in your family; religion, hearth, and heart; for treasure beyond wealth; for the Word and for wisdom that comes from being intertwined with others' lives more intimately than we can ever imagine. And this story is perfect for looking at Matthew's Gospel and the approaches to its interpretation as a source of wisdom, its insights of the Spirit, and its call to conversion. "Dig Deeper" is always the injunction, always the practice.

There are three turning points or angles in the story. The first is the soldier's laughter and then his sharing of his dream that turns the man back to his own hearth after his long journey in response to his own dream. This dialogue provides the essential groundwork for anything that will happen. The second turning takes place when the man gives up and his children find the treasure, imitating him. Others often unexpectedly find what we have been searching for, and share their findings with us. And the third transpires when the man and woman decide to give their last coin to the beggar, who gives them the wisdom of "Dig Deeper!" The beggar is the messenger or angel that brings the Word of God to them because of their generosity and trust. These three turning points catch you off-guard and spring the story into different directions, changing everything each time.

Likewise, there are three elements to remember when reading the Gospel of Matthew. Its historical context contains three issues that provide the background for Matthew's Gospel. These are also theological realities essential to understanding those in Matthew's community and their need for a gospel that would teach them, draw them forth on their journey, call them to conversion and witness to their belief in the world.

The gospel was probably written in the 80s, after the destruction of the Temple in Jerusalem. This was a time of painful division between the Jewish and Christian communities and between the people of the Jewish nation and their leadership, hard realities to absorb and live with gracefully. This is the first aspect of the context in which Matthew wrote his Gospel. His primary audience is Jewish, and the Jews are experiencing painful, even violent separation from their roots, their families, their traditions, economies, and their shared identity as Jews. Excluded and isolated from their Jewish pasts, who are they? The separation is causing tension and anger between the leadership of the Jews and the leadership of the Christian communities.

At the same time the community of Christians is growing, expanding out among the Gentiles, bringing richness and new grace, new converts, the next generation, but also disagreements, factions, and dissension. Jews and Gentile converts to Christianity fight among themselves on how to live together and how to practice what the Spirit has given them in the words and practice of Jesus.

Third, Roman persecution causes distress, fear, and insecurity within a community struggling to be faithful to the teachings of Jesus. So much of what Jesus was, said, and did contradicts everything that Rome stands for and tries to impose upon their lives. In imitating and following their Master, the Christian community faces danger, just as Jesus did with the Empire and its leaders.

So a new people is being born, one with Jewish roots and origins — yet a Gentile experience of Jesus, with an experience of the Spirit's presence and power — old yet new. Matthew writes his Gospel to give this new people an identity. It is thought that in these words Matthew describes himself: "Every scribe who has been instructed in the kingdom of heaven is like the head of a household who brings from his storeroom both the new and the old" (Mt 13:52). This is Matthew, as he sees himself and what he is attempting to do for his own household of Christians caught between past Jewish history and their hopes amid the Roman domination and power of the present. These Christians find themselves living a new reality, a new creation, the fullness of tradition given to them for all time in the person of Jesus Christ — prophet, new Moses, law and Spirit giver, liberator, sage, wisdom and Word made flesh among us, Son of Man and Son of God, risen from the dead and with us still in hidden glory, Emmanuel and "I Am." It is a hard place, yet one filled with grace, freedom, and Spirit as these early Christians become more truthfully the followers of Jesus in history.

These historical realities intrude into their lives as Christians and reverberate among their internal relationships. How do they remain together, how do they deal with disagreements, how do they sustain belief, growth, and expressions of worship and practice? What is authority in light of Jesus' teaching? How should it be exercised? Who is a teacher and what are Jesus' primary teachings? And running over and under and through all of these questions is how to maintain the community — how to keep it together despite the inner turmoil caused by events in the Jewish world and the Roman world.

Matthew's Gospel will meld his community together, keep it together and help its members to live gracefully under duress with one strong, vibrant, and unflinching imperative that lies at its core: God is the God of mercy. Mercy is made real in the practices of Forgiveness, Reconciliation and Atonement (meaning "at-one-ment," the community made one) and Restoration (meaning to repair the broken pieces, to make restitution so that the community can again be whole, holy).

This is the core, the heart of Matthew's Gospel and Matthew's Jesus. This is what Matthew exhorts in every word of the text and what he emphasizes in his stories and accounts. The new Christian, firmly rooted in Jesus' Jewish background of Torah and law, tradition and hopes, is open to the Spirit of the new that encompasses all peoples and demands that we treat one another as God now relates to us in Jesus.

Perhaps the familiar parable of the sheep and the goats epitomizes this best, when the Son of Man renders final judgment upon all the nations of the world "Amen I say to you, whatever you did for one of these least brothers of mine, you did for me" (Mt 25:40). The awesome mystery of the Incarnation lays the foundation for all our behavior with one another — what we do to one another, or what we ignore and do not do on behalf of others, we do to God, or we refuse to do for God. This has deep implications for each believer and for the community at large, in its communal practice and internal relations. And it is all the more difficult, and yet necessary, for the community to do this consistently, consciously, in the power and grace of the Spirit in the face of persecution, fear, insecurity, dissension, and differences as it struggles to emerge as a distinct entity, as its individual members strive to become disciples of Jesus, his household, bringing his kingdom of God upon the earth in history now.

Matthew's Gospel is about the emerging church, about the household of God. It is dedicated to uncovering the kingdom of God upon earth and bringing this good news of the presence of God to the entire world. This community is very like a hermit crab outgrowing its shell, cracking and breaking as it struggles to free itself, totally vulnerable to potentially hostile surroundings while it seeks a new shell to dwell within. Each individual must go through this stripping and growth, but they do it within a community that is seeking to create something new, conceived by the Spirit in the life, death, and resurrection of Jesus, to the glory of the Father. And this Trinitarian foundation suffuses the gospel. Many of its sections end with a prayer to the Father, a reference to the Father, Son, and the Holy

Spirit, or both. The actual baptismal formula of inclusion and initiation into the Trinity appears for the first time in the final words of the last chapter of Matthew's Gospel (28:16–20). This chapter and Jesus' parting exhortation to his followers, now his friends, concerning what they are to do in the world. This is often considered the linchpin of the gospel itself. It reads:

> The eleven disciples went to Galilee, to the mountain to which Jesus had ordered them. When they saw him, they worshiped, but they doubted. Then Jesus approached and said to them, "All power in heaven and on earth has been given to me. Go, therefore, and make disciples of all nations, baptizing them in the name of the Father, and of the Son, and of the Holy Spirit, teaching them to observe all that I have commanded you. And behold, I am with you always, until the end of the age."

In the past, scripture scholars have considered this emerging community as consisting primarily of the disciples — the twelve who became apostles, later, the eleven — together with the leadership styles and choices of the Jewish community. In recent years, however, some scholars have shifted their focus to others who represent the new disciple in Matthew's community, looking at the margins and the people who walk those margins — Gentiles, beginning with the Magi from the east, then the Roman centurion who seeks a cure for his servant, and the Canaanite woman who begs healing for her daughter. In addition, there are the many "unclean" Jews who Jesus touched and healed, and so were drawn into the community: a leper, Peter's mother-in-law, the man possessed in the country of Gadara, a paralytic, the woman with a hemorrhage, the two blind men, a dumb demoniac, the man with the withered hand, the epileptic boy, the crowds at large who are described as distressed, and even the city of Jerusalem itself for which and over which Jesus weeps. The scribes, the Pharisees, the priests, and Jewish elders are foils — those who reflect what the community and its leaders are not to imitate, because if they do, they bring about

their own demise and condemnation. We can read and reflect upon
the stories of the Jewish leaders, in contrast to those in need
who approach Jesus, desperate for his attention, his acceptance,
and touch. These people, not the Jewish leadership, characterize
Matthew's community.[1]

But three other people in Matthew's Gospel also stand at the
center of the image and practice of discipleship. They are Joseph,
the husband of Mary; Peter, the disciple who becomes the leader of
the larger Christian community; and Joseph of Arimathaea, who
will bury Jesus in his own tomb. These three men mirror what it
means to be a new disciple of the new creation in the new kingdom
of God upon earth now, in history. And surprisingly it is Joseph, the
legal father of Jesus, who is the one to imitate, not Peter. Peter is the
foil — a contrast in behavior, who, with his lack of understanding
and obedience, needs to be taught and re-taught and constantly
pulled along into a new awareness of who Jesus is and what it means
to imitate him with the Spirit that permeates the law, with the hope
of the old and the promise of the new fulfilled in practice and deci-
sion-making now, and the drawing into the very heart of the community the outcast, the sinner, the sick and the marginalized, the
despised. It is Joseph of Arimathaea who slowly goes through the
process from being a Jew, then a Jewish believer in Christ, and
finally a Christian.

Some think that just as Luke used the persona of Mary as a theological model for the catechumenate in his own community and how

---

1. Some have described the tone of Matthew's words against the leaders of the
   Jewish community as anti-Semitic, but in fact such conflict between the two
   groups did occur. Sadly, with time such statements in the gospel, taken out
   of their historical context, were used to condemn the Jewish people, a reality
   for which the church has in the recent past sought to apologize and make
   amends, specifically with John Paul II's words of sorrow to the Jewish community for the past wrongs the church has committed against them. In reality, however, at the time of the gospel's composition Christians did distrust
   and feel betrayed by some Jews, and the two groups and their leaders did feel
   anger and did distance themselves from one another.

a new believer was initiated into belief and the sacraments, Matthew uses her husband, Joseph, as the model of a believer — a Jew who in the power of the Spirit interprets the law for life, obeys the Word of the Lord, practices love, intimacy, and protection of those who are vulnerable, and possesses the wisdom of God, struggling to act as God wills in the face of tradition, culture, family, and religious laws. The next chapter will look at Jesus' origins and at Joseph, who is the first to hear the gospel and put it into practice in his own life, making moral decisions and living ethically according to the Spirit of the law.

Matthew's Gospel is filled with parables — teaching stories and segments that are presentations or collections of sayings on practice. They constitute five discourses: the Sermon on the Mount (including the Beatitudes); the initial proclamation of the coming of the kingdom of God into the world in the person and presence of Jesus; the mission sermon; the parable collection; a presentation of in-house church practices on forgiveness, reconciliation, authority, and communion; and the last sermon on judgment.

The Jewish people had based their lives on the Temple, the Torah, the Land, and the Promises of a Messiah to come. At the time of Matthew's writing, the Temple is utterly destroyed, the Jews live in occupied territory under the Roman Empire's rule, and the Torah (the first five books of the Bible), the Prophets, and the Law become central to understanding what makes a Jew and what constitutes being holy while they wait for the Messiah to come.

Moreover, Matthew's Jewish/Gentile/Christian community takes a new direction by believing that Jesus is the long-awaited Messiah and so much more — the beloved child of God, the Son of Man, Emmanuel, God-with-us. The Torah, the Word of God, and the Law are still central to both communities. But Jesus has deepened the law, altered it to serve the least, and extended it outside the Jewish community to all peoples, even to enemies. Jesus' own behavior, parables, and teaching discourses seek to lay a foundation for a fresh and demanding interpretation and practice of the law, infusing it with a new Spirit of Mercy, of love unto death, of universality, a lifestyle of remembering one's own need of forgiveness and conversion, now extended perpetually to others — all others, all the time, in all areas of life. Matthew's Jesus is the best of the Hebrew Scriptures — the new Moses, the lawgiver and liberator, the new sage and Wisdom of God, the new prophet whose Word both castigates in judgment and heals and accepts in forgiveness and touch; the Messiah who fulfills all the hopes and prophecies of the past, but in ways that are so radically other than expected. He is not political or nationalistic, and he understands and exercises his authority and power unlike any other authority and power among nations and leaders. It is an authority of prophetic truth tempered with understanding and graciousness. It is an authority universal and equal among all peoples, with no distinctions between man or woman, rich or poor, Jew or Gentile, clean or unclean. And it is an authority based on humility, service, and ways of acting that serve always to preserve communion and unity within the church. It is the authority and power of Mercy incarnate, God-with-us, Emmanuel, Jew, Son of David, human, and yet the Christ, the Messiah, the Son of Man and Son of God, the new hope of the human race and of all time. And Matthew's Gospel will be part of the New Testament, the new covenant, the new Spirit, the new presence of God among the people.

"Dig Deeper" reminds us how to read the Gospel of Matthew. It is a treasure old and new, and we must dig into, immerse ourselves in the scriptures of the Jewish community, dig to the core, to Jesus, to Christianity, to being holy as is God who is Trinity. Matthew will constantly revert to scripture passages, the prophets, the original books of Moses, and the law as it develops over a thousand years. All the people's hopes of the past burst forth in the person of Jesus. Digging deeper is foundational. Jesus tells his disciples and us: "Do not think that I have come to abolish the law of the prophets. I have come not to abolish but to fulfill [or complete them]" (Mt 5:17). The gospel is about completing, making whole and extending the wisdom and knowledge of the past through the person and words of Jesus.

And Matthew's Gospel is a dream — a vision into the future, often called the vision of the kingdom of God come among us now, a vision that is to pervade all the world, all of history, and is to serve as hope for all nations. This is part of Jesus' own prayer that he teaches those who wish to dwell in the kingdom of God now on earth. It is the first thing and in some ways the only thing that we pray for, as brothers and sisters to Jesus, to the Father, in the grace of the Spirit.

> Our Father in heaven,
> hallowed be your name,
> your kingdom come,
> your will be done,
> on earth as in heaven. (Mt 6:10)

We participate in the task and the honor of bringing this kingdom ever more surely into being and making the will of God a reality for all, a symbol of hope and justice, of mercy and love, for all to see and be heartened. We do this by witnessing to the presence of the kingdom (the presence of Jesus among us, and our new relationship to God the Father in Jesus through the Spirit) by obeying all that we have been commanded, and in our dealings with others being the visible and tangible presence of God.

And we must dig ever deeper into the older texts, the scriptures of Matthew's Gospel and into our own lives, individually and as communities of believers, to understand and garner wisdom. And we must dig deeper into our world, our history, our culture, and our relationships with other groups to get to the truth of what we are called to be in the world. We must convert ourselves and our communal life, to give an alternative of hope to the ways of the world. And the church, universally and locally, must stand in resistance to the empires of our day. We must search through the old and discard what is destructive and demeaning, what isolates and condemns, and dig deeper into the Word of God in both the earlier and the newer Testaments to find the Spirit that heals, that gives hope, that includes all, that forgives and reconciles and keeps all in communion. We, as believers and as church, must witness to the world authority and power as Jesus practiced and taught

— true authority and power, deeper than any found in nations or even in religion itself and that serves all humbly, that only judges one's brothers and sisters as we are judged, and that loves and loves and loves and does not exclude, condemn, or cast out but only treats others as we seek to be treated. We must dig deeper into the text of the Word of God to find a new standard more demanding yet more freeing than the old one, and we must dig deeper into our own lives to be converted to that standard — to become the salt of the earth and the light of the world (see Mt 5:13–14). Our own communion and unity must be a haven, a sanctuary, an invitation to the kingdom of God upon the earth.

Approaching the Word of the Lord, inspired by the Spirit in the Gospel of Matthew, we must be prepared to be taken off-guard, surprised and turned around. The gospels are written to convert us ever anew, to encourage us to dig deeper into our own souls and lives to become the words that we read and reflect upon with others in community. We must know and understand the text that tells us how to imitate God in Jesus, but we must also become holy as our God is holy, in deeds, and in truth, for all to see and give glory to God — and to question our own lives and wonder about this Jesus that we seek to follow and reflect.

A teaching story among the rabbis suggests the attitude we must seek if we are to practice, individually and in community, what we learn from the scriptures. And it reminds us that we must encourage each other in this endeavor to be the kingdom and be the holiness of God for others:

> * Once upon a time, a group of scholars of the law came to visit the rabbi of Viedislav. The rabbi was very proud of his young son, Simcha, who was only five but whom he had taught and tutored from his birth. The rabbi and the boy loved the Torah[2] and were always playing word puzzles about the daily portion, as they read and studied and played games about how to inter-

---

2. From the root word *yaroh,* meaning a teaching or an instruction.

pret it in new and diverse ways — relying on the older sages and their interpretation but taking it further and further into their own lives. When the men arrived, the rabbi himself prepared them a meal, treating them as honored guests.

While they were eating and talking of issues dear to the Jewish community and what was going on in the world, the rabbi called his son to him, and in the presence of all the guests told his son that he had a game for him. "While our guests are eating, please go and prepare some new interpretation of the laws of hospitality so that when we are finished you can share it with all of us." And the boy brightened, smiled at the challenge, and went off to work on the project.

The boy was gone awhile but came back to the table before they finished eating. The other rabbis were surprised. That was quick work at an interpretation of a law and concept central to the heart of Jewish living and practice! His father smiled at him. "Are you ready?" And the boy smiled back and nodded. But he told his father, "I'd rather not share it now. We had best wait until everyone has finished." They ate the rest of their meal and drank their wine, wondering what the young child had come up with and curious to see how he would explain something innovative and yet true to the tradition, and he was only five!

When their long conversations concluded and no more food remained, it was time for Simcha to present his work. He gathered the rabbis and told them, "I don't have anything to say really, but instead I want to show you something. Please come with me." They got up from the table and followed the young boy through the house. In each of the rooms, the study, the extra room, the library, he had prepared a bed for each of the guests, with clean sheets, blankets, pillows and a quilt, a pitcher of water and a glass, and a candle-holder. They looked at one another and asked Simcha, "What is so new about your interpretation?" The boy looked at them, surprised. "Teachers," he spoke, "with all due respect, if I had used words, even new words, you would only have found rest and refreshment for your minds — and you've had that since you came to our house and sat at our dinner table talking with each other. Instead I decided to do something to help you rest your bodies and your hearts as well. You will be comfortable here for the night and you will be able to go home fully refreshed."

They stood in silence, wondering at the boy's words and his deeds, and his father stood smiling, thoroughly pleased with his son, who already knew that it is more important to act upon belief and put thoughts into action. Or as the sages would say: "It is more important to be like God, blest be His Name, than to know and speak about Him."

This is the way we can approach Matthew's Gospel and our reading and study of it together. The church of Matthew sought to honor the old that was their heritage and hope, and at the same time to incorporate the new they had received from Jesus — the words, the wisdom and knowledge and all that these demanded, the unbelievably new presence and understanding of God among them. It was an adventure of light and freedom, of forgiveness and mercy, of grace in the Spirit and a way of life that would form them into something new — Christians, God's presence on earth, a sanctuary for all, especially for those most in need, for the poorest, for those seeking the holiness of God. It would take them away from what had been their treasure, but they would retain what was best as they created a new way of living and of interpreting the Word of God. They would dream the dreams of the Spirit of Jesus and make them come true in their lives knowing they, as did Jesus, would experience resistance from other authorities and powers in building the kingdom of God on earth. But they would dig deeper into the Word made flesh in the scriptures of old and the Word ever new among them, in the community where the Spirit dwelt and in each of its members called to be salt and light for each other and the world. It was the beginnings of church, the beginnings of Christianity, the beginnings of the kingdom coming and the beginnings of the Spirit teaching the Body of Christ ever more deeply and truly. This gift is now given to us, the church to be made real on earth in the very year of the Lord in which we now live. It is time for us to go on our journey to find treasure, to dream and to dig deeper together and to become God's presence in the world today.

This book is intended not only for individual reading and study, but for groups and small communities that study the Word of God together throughout the cycle of readings during a liturgical season. Each chapter ends with a few questions that might help in reflecting upon the texts and the theology presented. It may also be used as background material for the portion of the gospel read at each Sunday's liturgy. The questions can be used with each scripture passage during group study. They have been used over the last forty years to make the scriptures come true in our own lives and to deepen awareness that we are not only to believe what we read, but to become what we believe, to incorporate in our flesh and blood and bone the Word of God given to us.

Questions

1. What does the scripture passage make me feel, or stir inside me?

2. What does the scripture passage say that is true? Who? What? When? How? Where? Why? What does it mean for my belief?

3. What in the scripture passage bothers me, disturbs me, or calls me to conversion and radical change?

4. After discussing these questions, what am I going to do in my own life this week to make the gospel come true?

5. We are made and called to be prophets by our baptism and confirmation in the community. What does this passage say we should be proclaiming prophetically together in the world?[3]

---

3. Prophets are interested in what constitutes true worship of God, what brings the kingdom of justice and peace, and what leads to the care of the poor. For prophets and for God these three are all one and the same thing. To bring the kingdom of peace and justice into the world cares for the poor and this is the only worship that God desires from us.

6. If what we proclaim as prophets is the Word of God for the world, then what does the scripture say we should do together to make this prophetic word a reality in our world today? (Usually this begins as one of the corporal works of mercy done together as witness to the gospel, then develops as the community takes action with others for justice, for peace.)

7. What in the scripture (the text itself, the Word of God) gives us hope and courage to change, to redeem situations and relationships, and to obey the Word of God that is given to us?

8. (If you are a part of an RCIA group or teaching group.) Use the text itself to make belief statements that can be shared as core teaching among those who are becoming Christians. For example, the text itself says that Jesus has come to complete the Law and the Prophets. A belief statement based on this text is that we must study the Old Testament to know and understand Jesus' deeper and more demanding interpretation of the Word of God. This is our Judeo-Christian heritage, as it was with Matthew's own community of believers.

Now we turn to the Gospel of Matthew and seek to incorporate it into our history and become this good news of the kingdom of God now among us.

2
The Origins of Jesus' Birth and Infancy Narratives

There is a beautiful and haunting story about someone who at the onset of war endeavored to save Jews in Germany.

* His name was Chiune Sugihara. He was one of the Japanese consuls, and against the orders of his own government he wrote out visas for thousands and thousands of Jews. He slid them under doors, threw them out train windows, passed them out on the street, doing as much as he could to help, with no thought of payment or of his own safety. After the war even his name was forgotten but as the children of those he saved grew up, it became clear how many he had saved, and he was to be recognized as one of the righteous Gentiles who contributed to the hope and life of the people of Israel.

Usually, a grove of cherry trees was planted to honor someone who had performed such a service, but when the extent of his work came to light it seemed right that something special had to be done for him. It was decided instead to plant a grove of cedar trees in his honor and memory. The connection between the Temple in Jerusalem and to the towering and graceful cedars of Lebanon seemed more apropos for all that he had done for the Jewish people. When Mr. Sugihara was notified that the grove had been planted, an amazing connection between what had happened in his life and in the

life of Israel came to light — his name, Sugihara, meant cedar
grove! This remarkable story, which I call "What's in a
Name?" is a fitting opening to the origins, naming, and birth of
Jesus in Matthew's Gospel.

The Gospel of Matthew does not begin at the birth of Jesus but
with Jesus' origins, with his ancestry and genealogy, going back to
the beginnings of faith, to Abraham and his son Isaac. This long line
will end with Joseph of the house of David, the earthly, legal father
of Jesus. This listing, this history of believers who lived on the Word
of God — the Torah — and its promises, is crucial to understanding
who Jesus is. He is the culmination of this nation, his race, and the
chosen people of Yahweh God. This is the Genesis of Jesus. As a
Jew Matthew thinks, breathes, and lives in the shadow and the light
of the Torah. Genesis first recounts creation, the beginnings of the
heavens and the earth, then the generations of humankind (see Gn 4
and 5). Just so, Matthew's Gospel begins with Jesus' own roots in
this people: "The book of the genealogy of Jesus Christ, the son of
David, the son of Abraham...." He is the offspring of all these
people. "Genealogy" signifies "origin," "beginnings." And Jesus
himself will generate and bring forth a new people of God, those
born again in his Spirit as his brothers and sisters, to the glory of our
one Father.

A careful reading of this genealogy reveals something unheard of in
the rendering of a Jewish person's lineage. It includes the names of five
women! Tamar, Rahab, Ruth (the wife of Uriah), and Mary — "Of her
was born Jesus who is called the Messiah" (Mt 1:16). Three of these
women are Jewish and two are outsiders — Gentiles or pagans. Each
provides a hint of something that will be important to Matthew's
readers — and a reminder that God has been at work in history since
the beginning, preparing Israel and the world for the coming of Jesus.
The first is Tamar, the wife of Er, who is the first-born son of Joseph's
elder brother, Judah. The poor woman loses Er, who was "wicked in
the sight of the Lord" and then by law is given in marriage to his
brother Onan. He takes her in marriage as the law dictated but he
wastes his seed rather than let her conceive a child, and also dies. Judah

breaks the law. He tells her to go back to her father as a widow, hoping to preserve his next son from having to be her husband. Tamar, however, knows the law and positions herself as a prostitute along the way that Judah will take when he goes to shear the sheep. She knows Judah too, it seems!

He falls for her ruse but has no money, so she demands his seal, his cord and his staff as pledges for future payment. Within three months the obviously pregnant Tamar is denounced, and Judah, as leader of the clan, decrees that she should be taken out and burned. When she returns his pledges he, of course, realizes whose child she is bearing and that she has caught him in violation of the law. As it turns out, Tamar was carrying twins: Perez and Zerah. Even through wiles and seduction, lust and betrayal, and the law both broken by and used to protect a woman who will bear children, the line of Judah continues (see Gn 38).

The second woman, the pagan prostitute Rahab, lives in the walls of Jericho when Joshua's scouts come to check the fortifications of the city before they attack. She hides them, but also makes a deal with them to save herself, her family, and all her relatives and kin. She tells them that she has "heard how the Lord dried up the waters of the Red Sea before you when you came out of Egypt ... since the Lord your God is God in heaven above and on earth below" (Jo 2:10–11). The scouts promise to spare her people, and when they come to attack the city she is to gather her family together in her house and to leave a scarlet cord hanging in her window. When the city falls to the Israelites, all of Rahab's family are spared. Her heroic story of allegiance to Israel's God Yahweh ends with the statement: "Because Rahab the harlot had hidden the messengers whom Joshua had sent to reconnoiter Jericho, Joshua spared her with her family and all her kin, who continue in the midst of Israel to this day" (Jo 6:25). This woman hears what God has done for Israel, hears and converts to Israel's God, putting her own life in danger to save her kin. There is secrecy and violence, but the word is heard and the word of the scouts is honored and kept and Rahab and her family are adopted into Israel.

Ruth has an entire book named after her. She is a Moabite, the widowed daughter-in-law of an Israelite, the widow Naomi. These two women of the poor, the *anawim* of God, decide to return to Bethlehem, for they have heard that Yahweh has given his people food there. Ruth vows to stay with Naomi, in faithful friendship. Ruth pleads to accompany Naomi home to support her, even though doing so meant going into exile. Her poignant words are often used for wedding vows: "Where you go, I will go; Where you lodge, I will lodge; your people shall be my people, and your God my God" (Ru 1:26). The two of them use the laws and customs of Israel to lure Naomi's cousin Boaz into meeting and marrying Ruth so that they will have a home together. After the harvest they glean, and Ruth sleeps in the field. At Naomi's instruction, she sleeps at the feet of Boaz and she becomes his wife. Ruth is given a blessing as she is drawn into the people of Israel: "May the Lord make this wife come into your house like Rachel and Leah, who between them built up the house of Israel. May you do well in Ephrathah and win fame in Bethlehem. With the offspring the Lord will give you from this girl; may your house become like the house of Perez, whom Tamar bore to Judah" (Ru 4:11–12). Ruth's first child, Obed, is the father of David's father, Jesse. And so the line continues unbroken.

The next woman is Jewish, but her actual name is never mentioned. She is only described by her relationship to her husband, Uriah, one of King David's trusted generals. But David has seen Bathsheba (this is a title that means "daughter of the oath," not an actual name) bathing, and lusts after her to be yet another of his wives. They conspire to have Uriah killed in battle so that David can marry her; they conceive a child but the boy soon takes sick and dies. The prophet Nathan confronts David on his scheming, his murder of Uriah and his collusion with Bathsheba to make her his wife and queen. Their child conceived in the blood of Bathsheba's husband dies, but as a gesture of Yahweh God's great forgiveness and peace, they are given another, Solomon, who will rule after David (see 2 Sm 11–12). It is noteworthy that Bathsheba names the child Solomon, but Yahweh has Nathan call the child Jedidiah. Later she and Nathan collude to assure that of David's many offspring her child will become the king in Israel (see 1 Kgs 1:1–40). The long-awaited one's lineage contains an odd assortment of sinners, murderers, those who scheme evil with others to ensure their place in history, politicians who misuse religion for their own ends rather than for the honor and worship of God. Like all of our human ancestors, they are a motley group.

And the last mentioned is the mother of Jesus: "… Jacob the father of Joseph the husband of Mary. Of her was born Jesus who is called the Messiah" (Mt 1:16). The stage has been set and the generations unfurled and now the time is fulfilled. What was begun in Abraham, the father of faith and the father of many nations, culminates in Joseph the husband of Mary, and a new and deeper faith is born. In the tradition of Judaism, Jewishness passes through the mother's lineage, but legitimacy through the father's. Joseph is the legal father of Jesus, a necessity in the history of Israel; through Joseph, Jesus is a son of David. But Jesus will be born of Mary — and of Yahweh God.

Here is the birth announcement delivered to Joseph shortly after Jesus' conception. Its one short paragraph contains the many images and theological symbols and themes essential to Matthew's Gospel itself and to coming to belief within Matthew's community, as well as to continual conversion to the Word of God. The passage also contains allusions to the first lines of the book of Genesis:

> Now this is how the birth of Jesus Christ came about. When his mother Mary was betrothed to Joseph, but before they lived together, she was found with child through the Holy Spirit. Joseph her husband, since he was a righteous man, yet unwilling to expose her to shame, decided to divorce her quietly. Such was his intention when, behold, the angel of the Lord appeared to him in a dream and said, "Joseph, son of David, do not be afraid to take Mary your wife into your home. For it is through the Holy Spirit that this child has been conceived in her. She will bear a son and you are to name him Jesus, because he will save his people from their sins." All this took place to fulfill what the Lord had said through the prophet:

"Behold the virgin shall be with child and bear a son, and
they shall name him Emmanuel," which means "God is
with us." When Joseph awoke, he did as the angel of the
Lord had commanded him and took his wife into his house.
He had not relations with her until she bore a son, and he
named him Jesus. (Mt 1:18–25)

This child is a son of David through Joseph, but more importantly
this child is the Son of God through the Holy Spirit. Jesus is the Son
of God at conception, unlike any previous ancestor who became son
of David at a coronation. Matthew uses the same word for Holy
Spirit found in the first lines of Genesis, when a strong and mighty
wind breathes and sweeps over the face of the deep. Just as the Spirit
of God created the heavens and earth, this child is created by the
breath of the Spirit of God sweeping over the face of Mary. This has
happened, and this is part of what is proclaimed to Joseph.

Joseph's Jewishness is essential to interpreting the depths and
layers of this passage. He is a good Jew, living in occupied territory
under the Romans, living on the promises and the Torah, both as the
Word of God and the law of Yahweh. Joseph "eats, sleeps and
drinks" the Word of God; he even "dreams" the Word of God. He
knows the law and that if his betrothed wife is pregnant it gives him
two choices. He can expose her to the full public horror of the law,
the strict interpretation of which would have her and her unborn
child stoned to death so that it will not be born. Or he can choose to
put her away "quietly" — divorce her ritually in the synagogue, and
put her aside, leaving her to bear her child and struggle to raise the
child outside the support of the community. He chooses what he
sees as the lesser of the two violent choices under the law, the more
lenient response that will allow Mary to live and the child to be born
— but at best their lives would be steeped ever after in humiliation,
exclusion and poverty. Joseph is described as "righteous," a man of
honor. The best translation of *tsaddiq,* the word used to describe
Joseph, is "a just man," "a man after God's own heart." No one can
be given a higher compliment. No one else in the New Testament is
so described. Joseph's justice, rooted in and born of the law, is inti-

mately connected with the scripture, the Word of God. And so in a dream an angel, a messenger of God, comes to him quoting scripture and telling him in essence to disobey the law and take Mary into his house as his wife; not only is he to protect the child, but he is to adopt him legally as his own.

This Joseph is named for his counterpart in the book of Genesis. The brothers of that Joseph, the second-youngest son of Jacob, describe him disparagingly: "Here comes that master dreamer!" (Gn 37:18). He is the first of the dreamers of God, a shepherd with visions of being a ruler. Sold into slavery by his brothers, then thrown into jail, he secures his release by interpreting dreams for the Pharaoh. When he rises to power, he saves not only his own brothers and aging father from famine, but also his entire people. Joseph forgives his brothers for all the harm they did to him and welcomes them, feasts with them, reunited with his youngest brother and their father. And 400 years later, when Moses takes the people to liberation in the Exodus, they take Joseph's bones along with them to the land of promise (see Gn 37–50).

Now this Joseph, the husband of Mary, is introduced by the command of the Word of God to the deepest and truest interpretation of any law: mercy that leads to life, ever more abundant for all involved, especially those most in need of life. The Word of God in scripture spoken in Joseph's dream by an angel is the basis for obedience to a command that seems to contradict everything in the custom and the tradition of the practice of the Law. This is the beginning of the Good News. This is the shadow that the very birth of this child casts upon the earth: the bright shadow of mercy. The Latin word is *misericordia* — a heart filled with pity or compassion. This is the basis of the new interpretation of all Law — compassion — suffering with another, and so easing their suffering by responding with unbounded, unpremeditated, tender concern, regard, and respect for the other person. Joseph is commanded to lay aside his plans — for marriage, children, family, and a place in the heritage and hope of Israel; but he is also commanded to acknowledge in public this child as his own, and to adopt Mary's child into the lineage of David. And so Joseph has mercy on Mary and the child to be born.

Joseph is called to an act of faith that for the rest of his life will affect his relationship with his wife Mary, his son whom the public will acknowledge as his first-born, and as a Jew, his understanding and practice of the law and what it means to be holy. This act of faith, this obedience to the Word of God proclaimed to Joseph is the first story of Incarnation, the first story of a person called beyond his understanding of what religion means to a profound new sense of obedience to the Word of God and the law. This is the model Matthew offers to all believers in his community — conversion in the depths of their beings to understand when to break a law and when to use the law to protect another, at the same time obediently surrendering one's own life and all the years to come to that Word and to a more demanding law. Joseph is the first to become a believer.

This Joseph draws his very life from the Word of the Lord. He chooses life over the law. Even though publicly disgraced in the community, Joseph the righteous, the holy, the just, loves life more than any law. This is law that liberates. In response to the Word of God Joseph declares with his actions that no one can ever again use the law, any law, to justify judgment or power, condemnation or control, over the life of another. From now on, when we hear the Word of God that comes to us in the scripture, with Joseph we must wait and watch, dream and imagine what God would have us do in the world in the service of life, in the service of love.

Joseph hears, and he will hear again and again: "Do not be afraid." This command liberates us all, frees each of us to search for life-giving, life-loving responses to every circumstance and condition the world presents. Joseph begins his new life by altering the law, by breaking it — this is the new righteousness and holiness of Joseph, and of the believers who follow Jesus. Joseph is the new man, a Christian from the moment he chooses to obey. The Word has given birth to Joseph as surely as the Word becomes flesh to dwell among us for all time. This is the new Wisdom of God, the Giver of life.

From the beginning, from the genesis of life, Joseph has lived under the long eye of God, as have we all. This is how we become more and more human, how our flesh takes on the Word of God in the world. And Joseph is the first to witness who this child is. The story about Chiune Sugihara that begins this chapter is titled, "What's in a Name?" This child is given three names: Jesus, Christ (or Messiah), and Immanuel, God-with-us. What's in a name? Everything is in the names. The name "Jesus" is repeated four times in this passage — "Jesus" is the Hellenized version of the Hebrew Joshua (*yesua,* a shortened form of *y hosua,* which means "God saves"). He will be named after the Joshua who first brought the people into the Promised Land. Joseph being told to name the child Jesus, he who "will save his people from their sins" is a shattering break with tradition as well. In Jewish culture women did the naming. Not so here. Joseph will do the naming, an honor extended because of his faith and his obedience to God.

From the beginning of the scriptures, God is the savior of his people, liberating them from Egypt, from bondage, from their own weakness and betrayals, their lack of faithfulness to the covenant, bringing them back from the Exile and slavery, giving them the hope and promises of the prophets. Yahweh God is a saving God and in this child Jesus God will now save all (not just the Jewish people, chosen from the beginning). This is God's work in the person of Jesus.

This is the name that the Judeo-Christian community will honor and strive to imitate and mirror ever more to others. Paul's letter to the Philippians contains the ancient hymn of praise:

> Have among yourselves the same attitude that is also yours
>   in Christ Jesus,
> Who, though he was in the form of God, did not regard
>   equality with God
> something to be grasped.
> Rather, he emptied himself, taking the form of a slave,
>   coming in human
> likeness; and found human in appearance,
> he humbled himself, becoming obedient to death, even
>   death on a cross.

> Because of this, God greatly exalted him and bestowed on
>   him the name that
> is above every name,
> that at the name of Jesus every knee should bend, of those in
>   heaven and on earth and under the earth,
> and every tongue confess that Jesus Christ is Lord, to the
>   glory of God
> the Father. (Phil 2:5–11)

The second name given the child is "the Christ," the anointed one
of God, the Messiah-*christos*. It is not so much a name as a title: "the
Christ, the Messiah of God." Christ is the fulfillment of all the words
of scripture, the promises and the hopes of the nation. He is the
long-awaited one, the Sun of Justice, whose name is peace, light, and
truth, the advent of the presence of God among his people as the
Prophet, the Word made flesh, the Word of God made flesh. Jesus'
origins are in Yahweh God, the Spirit of God, Creator and Sustainer of
all life acting in history, bringing humankind to this day. And so
Joseph is exhorted to take this child as his own, adopting the one born
of God and Mary into his home and raising him for the people, for the
world. The prayer Joseph might have said on behalf of all his people
from that day until the child is born comes from Isaiah: "Let the clouds
rain down the Just One and the earth bring forth a Savior" (45:8, as
found in the Roman Missal).

And the announcement by the angel, "The virgin shall be with child
and bear a son and they will name him Emmanuel … God is with us,"
uses a name that Isaiah had pronounced eight centuries before. This
child is the abiding presence with us of the Holy One. His origins go
back through the prophets and through the people, bringing all the
Word of Yahweh God to bear in his flesh. Joseph will give him his
personal name — Jesus — but this name from the history of the people,
Emmanuel, will reappear only in an allusion in the last line of the
last chapter of Matthew's Gospel, when after the resurrection Jesus
proclaims who he is to his own people. Jesus' last words in this gospel
are: "Know that *I Am with You* all days, even to the end of the age" (Mt
28:20). Jesus declares that he is *"I Am,"* and now *I Am* is with us for all
time, dwelling with us on earth. The child grown to be a mature man,

crucified and raised from the dead will proclaim for all peoples that he is God incarnate for all time, abiding with us. The seeds are planted clearly in the opening chapter.

One of the characteristic trademarks of Matthew's Gospel appears first in this story — he will interrupt or end a particular account or segment with the phrase "This is to fulfill what was written of old, or in the prophets" and then he will connect the present events to older realities, God's promises and statements spoken by the prophets. These quotes from earlier sources surface frequently, but at the same time Matthew will break the verbal patterns in the text by placing the quote in contrast to, or juxtaposition with what is being said and done. This is meant to throw us off guard, catch us and make us rethink, what is being said, who Jesus is, and what he is doing. And therefore we reconsider what we are to do, in believing in him, and in following him to the fulfillment of his destiny — the handing over of his life in death to the Father by handing over his Spirit, and the Father raising him from the dead to glory where he abides with us and in the Triune God.

The Gospel of Matthew is a story about Jesus' origins, not his birth. His birth is covered in one sentence, in fact only one clause of a sentence: "she bore a son; and he named him Jesus." Jesus is the adopted child of Joseph, and the Son of the Spirit, of Yahweh God. From the beginning nothing is as it seems to be — and this will continue throughout the gospel. Joseph awakes from sleep — a term often used to indicate a shift of awareness, a moment of insight and enlightenment, the acceptance of wisdom — and obeys the Word of God, breaking all the traditions and the law so that God's will might be done on earth in him, in Mary, in Jesus. God has become flesh. God dwells with us. The Maker of the Universe is here among us to save us, to liberate us from bondage, and to lead us to a kingdom of justice and abiding peace.

But God's divine intervention and expression of power in the world will immediately affect all kinds of people in the world. The balance of power has been shaken and shifted or, as Martin Luther King, Jr., said in his oft-quoted "Where do we go from here?" speech, "The arc of the moral universe is long but it bends toward justice."

The story Matthew recounts next is one found only in his gospel — a story of light, the star of the Magi from the east, and a story of blood — Herod's vicious reaction in the killing of children. The Word has spoken. The child is born. God is with us. And some very unlikely people on earth have seen the effect of God's work in a star in the heavens and seek to know and come to this child, the new king whose Light is rising upon the earth.

Although the story is familiar, we shrink from its violence and evil. Three Magi, sages of Persia (modern day Iraq or Iran) who study the night skies, have seen a star rise in the east. We refer to them as wise men, but they come to Jerusalem and approach Herod, a man known for his brutality, his insecurity, his killing even his relatives to secure his throne. This is not the way wise persons make inquiries. Perhaps they are knowledgeable in the ways of the world, science, astrology, history, but they lack wisdom in their seeking. Their effect on Herod, and then on the whole city of Jerusalem is "deeply disturbing," as many texts translate it. But Herod is shrewd and has long known how to use religion and those who are knowledgeable in law, scripture, and tradition to serve him, not God. He summons the chief priests and scribes of the people to ascertain where the Christ is to be born: "In Bethlehem of Judea," they reply, "and the prophet continues":

> And you, Bethlehem, land of Judah, are by no means least among the rulers of Judah, since from you shall come a ruler, who is to shepherd my people Israel. (Mt 2:6)

These words instill fear in the mind and heart of Herod but he dissembles well, and continues the sham of being interested in the child's birth and even wanting to go himself to worship the new king. Incredibly, the Magi do not catch the hatred and the intent of Herod, who ruthlessly opposed any opposition, let alone someone that he thought might subvert his position or take over as king. Herod is not finished collecting information. He learns from the Magi the exact date when they located the star and tells them to find out everything they can about the child. And they obey him.

They leave the city and after their long journey the star once again appears, moving forward and showing them the way. They are filled with delight, following the light to the Light of the World. And the star stops.

> ... and on entering the house they saw the child with his mother Mary. They prostrated themselves and they did him homage. Then they opened their treasures, and they offered him gifts of gold, frankincense and myrrh. And having been warned in a dream not to return to Herod, they departed for their own country by another way. (Mt 2:10–12)

They entered the house — this word, house, will figure strongly in Matthew's Gospel — his community being the household of God, the church. And they do the royal child homage, they worship. They open and present gifts that represent power, authority, and humanity (gold, the world's criterion of power; frankincense, the world's symbol of authority — we still pray, "Let our prayer rise like incense in your sight" at evening prayer; and myrrh, one of the spices used in the burial of kings). The Magi have given away, have sacrificed all they have and now that their hands are empty and hearts full they have gained wisdom. They have seen the Light, and in a dream they learn not to return to Herod. Once you have seen the Light, once you meet the child of God, you must change, turn and go back to your life, your world, by another route.

In the scriptures a dream is much like an angel or a star (the words and concepts are almost interchangeable). A dream instills or imparts knowledge essential to the life of humankind; those who receive it and obey stake their lives on it, though even if their lives depended on it they could not explain it to others. The Magi have the star and, after they have worshiped, the dream. In Joseph's dream an angel quotes the scriptures. For us, we have the Gospels, stronger by far than any star, or angel, or dream — for the Word is the living presence of God with us, as strongly as is the Eucharist. The Magi return to their countries with the Wisdom and the Light within them.

Matthew brackets his gospel, in Chapter 2 and in the last chapter, with violence, with political intrigue, with soldiers and murder — much as those in Matthew's community are bracketed with institutional, religious, political, and personal violence, sometimes directed at them as individuals. One must not be naive like the Magi in seeking wisdom. Their unwitting collusion with Herod gave him all the information he needed to wreak vengeance and horror when he realized that he had been tricked and the Magi weren't coming back to him. As individuals and as companions on the journey we must be careful not to fall into the trap of evil — in government, in nations, in institutions, even in religion — that will enable others to use what little we know to torture or destroy others, even the innocent. Matthew places the story of Herod at the beginning of his gospel as an unmistakable reminder that the power, authority, and presence of God among us threatens all earthly powers and authority. We take a clear stance and we must learn to respond wisely to violence in our midst.

Again in a dream the angel of the Lord comes to Joseph. He is told to flee into Egypt with his wife and the child and hide until it is safe to return. Sometimes the best response to evil is to run and hide, to disappear, to live in secrecy. Once again Joseph obeys immediately — that night the three of them became illegal aliens, refugees, immigrants, strangers fleeing to the land that once enslaved their people. Jesus' parents will know the same fear that the Israelites lived in bondage, but as God has acted before, the time will come when God tells Joseph to return to Judah. And the pattern of Matthew's quoting of Old Testament scripture reveals clearly what is happening and who this child is: "Out of Egypt I have called my son" (Ho 11:1). This passage originally referred to Moses, but Jesus is the new Moses. He too will follow in the footsteps of his ancestors in faith, but now it has been said — this is God's son!

With calculated fury, Herod uses his information, his military might, his fears to visit destruction and slaughter on anyone remotely connected with the child. Using the geography he learned from the scribes and chief priests, and the time frame he extracted from the Magi, he makes himself feel secure by killing all boys two years old or younger. This too, echoes the slaughter of the boy children in the beginning of Exodus, when a Pharaoh who does not know Joseph comes to power and begins to exterminate the male offspring of the Israelites. Again scripture echoes with lamentation at senseless violent death:

> A voice was heard in Ramah, sobbing and loud lamentation; Rachel weeping for her children, and she would not be consoled, since they were no more. (Jer 31:15)

The story is wrapped in misery, in wanton destruction and hatred. Herod's reaction to the birth of the child has none of the sweetness found later in Luke's theological presentation. For the majority of those born into the world this is reality and it will be reality for those born into the Light and the Wisdom of the child who is God's presence with us. For now, the child escapes Herod's wrath but that shadow lies over him from his birth — so many have died in Herod's quest to kill him. And the day will come when the same forces — nation, religion, those who seek profit from power — will plot together and demand Jesus' death. In Matthew, whenever the leaders gather, they gather to do harm, and to protect their own interests.

Matthew's story of Jesus' origins ends with a sojourn in Egypt and with another of Joseph's dreams, this time giving him the relieving news that it is safe now to return to Israel. For now, those who sought to kill the child are themselves dead. But Joseph also has learned wisdom, and when he hears that Herod Archelaus, Herod's equally ruthless son, had succeeded his father as king, he returns instead to Galilee. The phrasing of the text is important: "But when he heard that Archelaus was ruling over Judea in place of his father Herod, he was afraid to go back there. And because he had been warned in a dream, he departed for the region of Galilee. He went and dwelt in a town called Nazareth, so that what had been spoken through the prophets might be fulfilled: 'He will be called a Nazarene' " (Mt 2:21–23). Wisdom is a blend of dreams and common sense, knowledge of the world as well as knowledge of the scriptures. And once again Matthew inserts his trademark to explain more of Jesus' origins and how he came to be in Nazareth. The great leader of the people, Samson was a simple man, also a Nazorean from the back country of Galilee. The connections continue, every detail fraught with meaning.

After this return to Israel the narration contains a lapse of three decades. We never hear of Joseph again. No more dreams. No more is said of how Jesus grew, matured, and became a man. Yet within the Jewish tradition it would have been Joseph, not Mary, who taught him. As soon as he was weaned he would have joined the men of the community and learned the rituals, the prayers, and the law from his father and the other men. And at twelve he would have had his bar mitzvah and assumed in the Jewish community the standing of an adult male. The gospel later reveals that Joseph is a carpenter, and scholars surmise that he settled in Nazareth of Galilee because of the available work in Sepporis, about four miles away, where Herod was building one of his cities, a twelve-year building project that demanded build-ers, bricklayers, and carpenters. As soon as Jesus could walk and carry tools, he would have gone with his father to work six days of the week. Jesus would have grown up honoring the Sabbath in the synagogue of his people and building a Jewish city within the Roman Empire.

The gospel later reveals more of Jesus' family when he visits Naza-reth as an adult and teaches in the synagogue of his youth:

> He came to his native place and taught the people in their synagogue. They were astonished and said, "Where did this man get such wisdom and mighty deeds? Is he not the carpenter's son? Is not his mother named Mary and his brothers James and Joseph and Simon and Jude? Are not his sisters all with us? Where did this man get all this?" And they took offense at him. But Jesus said to them, "A prophet is not without honor except in his native place and in his own house." And he did not work many mighty deeds there because of their lack of faith. (Mt 13:53–58)

Jesus is thought to have had the knowledge of a laborer, like his father, or the skills of a builder, stone mason, and carpenter, again like his father. He is known by his family relations, some by name, at least four brothers and two sisters. The people in his hometown think they know him yet they know nothing of him — they did not even know his real family. His origins are not in Nazareth or among his kin, but in God. Joseph knows this and has obeyed, adopting this child of God as his own, making him part of the people of Israel. In the above passage Jesus sees himself as a prophet, one who bears the Word of God in his mouth and speaks only the Truth of God. But his own disdain and reject him. By the time Jesus begins preaching as an itinerant prophet, Joseph is dead.

In Matthew's telling, when he appears at the very end of Jesus' theological family tree, Joseph is probably at most 14 or 15 years old, betrothed to Mary who would have been considered an adult at twelve; they have not yet moved in with each other, and they still reside in their parents' homes. So far we have looked at Joseph's place in Jesus' genealogy, but we haven't said much about Mary. There is one remarkable thing to say — leading us away from the concentration often put on her as an individual person, separate from all other human beings, especially from all other women. In his book *The Story Goes; Mark's Story and Matthew's Story,* Nico ter Linden writes of the symbolic value of the number of women in the genealogy: "Mary is by now the fifth woman to appear in this genealogy. From ancient times the figure five has stood as a symbol for Israel, for it's Israel's calling to proclaim the One God to all the four corners of the earth. One plus four is five. Mary is the fifth woman. Here she stands for the people Israel. She's a woman of Israel. She will give birth to the Messiah" (168).

The history of Israel is marked by remarkable births — mainly barren women at turning points in history who conceive by the power of God. In many of the surrounding countries kings, emperors and other dignitaries claimed that they had been fathered by deities and given birth by virgins. Even for Israelites this isn't as far-fetched as it may sound. When the kings were crowned in Israel, Psalm 2 would have been sung: "You are my son, today I am your father." In Matthew's mind the Spirit is piecing together all the old phrases from Isaiah and the other prophets to make remarkable statements — beyond any fundamentalist interpretation or simplistic rendering. Matthew is not predicting the future; he is doing theology for his community and telling them this royal child is unlike any royalty in history. Like Joseph of old, like Moses, like David, he will shepherd his people Israel, but in a way bound by mercy, by truthfulness, and by the power of God.

To refer again to Nico ter Linden, he explains the significance of Joseph naming Jesus, something even more important than the account of Jesus' birth. "In the biblical sense life doesn't begin when the first breath is drawn; life begins when your name is called out. The name expresses your being, your calling; it's the name by which you are called. You truly live only when you receive the name by which you can be called in this life" (172).

What's in a name? We have looked at the names revealed to Joseph about Jesus. But what of Joseph — what does his name mean? Joseph means "God will add or increase."

When the Joseph of Genesis interprets the dreams of Pharaoh and rises to power, he is given an Egyptian name: Zaphenath-paneah. Some suggest that it is derived from his Hebrew name and means "to hide" or "to elucidate," thus signifying "revealer of hidden things." In Egyptian, it means "God speaks; he lives." Rabbi Samson Raphael Hirsch suggests that the name could mean "he with whom the most secret things are kept." This is Joseph. The first book of Samuel teaches: " … he is just like his name" (1 Sm 25:25). A name bears the past and suggests the future to come in the reality of now. Joseph truly interprets dreams and secrets. Joseph is one to whom God speaks and when Joseph obeys God, the people are saved from death. This is true of Joseph the husband of Mary and his namesake, Joseph of Genesis.[1]

I will end this chapter concerning Jesus' origins and concerning Joseph, his father on earth who is a model for those initiated into belief with an old story about another Joseph, a carpenter, which illustrates what Matthew is trying to teach those who would be followers of Jesus.

---

1. Notes from "A Taste of Torah: Commentary from the JTS Community," 23 December 2006/ 2 Tevet 5767, on Genesis 41:1–44:1 by Rabbi Matthew L. Berkowitz.

* Once upon a time — it was in the hard times when the people of
Israel had lost the Ark of the Covenant — they were ruled over
by Judges but the unruly tribes were hard to manage and to keep
together. Without the Ark there was no place to gather, no place
for the power of God to draw their hearts into one. Worship in
other places just didn't seem to give the people strength or
enduring grace. The priests gathered and decided that since they
were no closer to finding the Ark than before they must make a
new one. And they decided to have a contest — to ask all the
tribes to summon their best carpenters, builders, and artisans to
build an ark. Then they would all gather as a people and the
priests would cast lots to see which one Yahweh God would
choose as the one that delighted Him most.

And so the people bent themselves to the task, approaching
it as worship. They gathered the best materials and their artists
and carpenters worked for months. Finally the day came for
the rite of acceptance and the people gathered, bringing the
arks with them. Each of the arks displayed astounding artistry,
craftsmanship, detail of work, and exquisite materials. They
were made of bronze and silver, a few of gold inlaid with
jewels, many of wood, cedar, balsam, myrtle. Some were
simple and others had ornate carvings, some even telling the
stories of the glorious deeds Yahweh God had done for his
people. The people moved around the arks in awe, wondering
which one Yahweh God would choose as his resting place
among his people. They watched as the high priest went from
one to another, casting his die, but one after another was
rejected. The tension arose among the people.

Then the high priest came to an ark to which no one had
paid much attention. It was simple, but finely worked. It
lacked detail or ornamentation. The sweet-smelling wood was
sanded fine. This ark had been crafted by Joseph, a carpenter
known not for his work, but for his devotion to the Torah and
his obedience to the law. When the die was cast, this ark
was accepted. The people and the other artisans and carpenters were dismayed. What? Yahweh God rejected all their
offerings and sacrifices and hard work, even the gifts and

talents that he had given them, in favor of this, this box? Again they demanded that the high priest throw the die and once again it was accepted. And again, a third time, the same ark, Joseph's Ark, was accepted. It was not any of the others but Joseph's Ark that Yahweh God wanted. The people remained angry and dismayed, then in their midst a prophet cried out in a loud voice: "This is the ark that I chose. With all the others, my people will stand admiring the workmanship and the craft and studying the details but with Joseph's Ark they will only be thinking of me, and calling on me and worshiping me. Joseph's Ark is my dwelling place among you."

And so it was. And so it was at the time of Jesus coming into the world. It was Joseph's Ark, Joseph's soul, and Joseph's life that Yahweh God chose. And so it is with us as well.

Questions

1. What is your name? What does it mean? Were you named after someone in your family, or a friend, or a famous person?

2. Are you becoming what your name means? Do you have other names that people call you? Who gave you those names and what do they mean to you?

3. When you were born, what violent realities were happening in human history and in natural history? Have they impacted your life?

4. When you pray to Jesus, what name do you usually call him? What does this say about your relationship to Jesus? What are you becoming as you pray and grow in understanding about who Jesus is?

3
The Treasure of
the Kingdom of God

After the chilling news of children being slaughtered and the lamentation of their mothers and fathers, Matthew's Gospel jumps ahead three decades to the desert where we meet John the Baptist, the preacher of repentance, warning that God's kingdom is "close at hand"! At the Jordan River John offers a baptism of repentance and to our amazement, he baptizes Jesus! But first let us consider a parable about baptism — the waters of life that wash out our eyes, ears, and hearts so we can see and hear the Word of God in Jesus.

* Once upon a time an old man wandered through towns and villages. In one he scratched a map on the plaza stones saying: "I have found the waters of life. Here is where you can find them." Many ignored what he wrote, but many copied the map and set out to find such waters. The first was a soldier coming home from the wars. He craved forgiveness and a way of life that would wash away his memories of battle. He found the waters easily enough, but was surprised that they were in a cave and that he would have to get on his hands and knees to enter. After a moment he stripped off his armor and piled it aside with his sword and shield. He crawled into the cave, and drank, and washed his face, and hands. When he emerged, he knew what he must do — he buried his armor and weapons, and clad only in a tunic walked away, intent on undoing the

harm he had done. No longer a warrior, he was free to make amends and restitution. He walked in peace.

Next came a woman of erudition who had studied languages, science, and mysticism. The waters of life intrigued her. In the pockets of her long dress and cape she carried her treasures: crystals, notes, candles, and herbs. She too felt appalled that she would have to crawl through the mud to enter the cave. But she wanted those waters. She stripped, wrapped up her clothing, and hid it in the bushes. She entered, knelt, drank deep, then washed. When she emerged she too knew what she had to do. She donned her clothes, but cut the long sleeves, cape, train, and hood to make clothes for others. She realized that her knowledge had no value unless used to ease others' lives and give them meaning.

Next came a rich husband and wife. Expecting to pay handsomely for the waters of life, they had loaded their pockets and sacks with jewels and coins. They too realized that to reach the waters they would have to leave everything outside. They piled their clothes and all their riches and crawled in, then drank and washed. They returned into the light with the new realization that wealth had to be shared. At first they dropped a coin here or a jewel there, but soon realized they had to use their possessions more shrewdly. They divested themselves of their riches and lived a life of extreme generosity to the poor.

Last came a bishop adorned in miter, gloves, cape, and vestments. He too shed his finery and bent on hands and knees to drink and to wash. When he emerged the sight of his trappings shocked him. He burned them, realizing power is meant to serve truth, authority to protect people, and ritual to free others to worship.

Many others came to the cave, stripped, and went in to drink. They emerged in the sunlight, put their clothes back on, and thought about what had happened but went back to their lives unchanged. Even though they thought about what they should do differently, how to live more truthfully, they did not let the sense that pushed at them convert or transform them.

Drinking and washing in the waters of life was enough. But they didn't realize that they were still slaves — they hadn't grasped what the waters of life offered. They returned to lives still bound in fear, insecurity, and selfishness. They did not realize the freedom of being children of God or the unequaled power of bending and worshiping God, of signing themselves with the cross, of spending their lives resisting weakness by divesting themselves of their possessions and sharing with others.

Still today, many seek the waters of life, drink, and wash, yet do not let freedom flood over them and draw them into the kingdom of God here on earth, sharing their gifts and living lives fresh and graceful after kneeling in the presence of the Lord. And you? Have you been baptized? Do you live now in the freedom of the children of God? Or do you think that to drink and to wash is enough to be saved? Are you a slave, or free?

Many come to John and his baptism of repentance, but he attacks them saying: " 'You brood of vipers! Who warned you to flee from the coming wrath? Produce good fruit as evidence of your repentance. And do not presume to say to yourselves, "We have Abraham as our father." For I tell you, God can raise up children to Abraham from these stones' " (Mt 3:8–9). Without a corresponding response of body, heart, mind, and soul as offering and sacrifice to God, ritual remains empty. John prepares the people for the one who will come with the Holy Spirit and fire. If they do not change attitude and action, they cannot see and hear the Word of God in Jesus. Jesus comes to John to be baptized, modeling for all believers how to become the Beloved children of God by letting ourselves be changed at our very roots after the sacrament. The lines of people wanting John to baptize them mark the beginning of the kingdom, the emergence of Jesus into a public life and the source of his power and authority to teach, to preach, to heal and to judge:

> After Jesus was baptized, he came up from the water, and behold, the heavens were opened (for him), and he saw the Spirit of God descending like a dove [and], coming

upon him. And a voice came from the heavens saying,
"This is my Beloved Son, with whom I am well pleased."
(Mt 3:16–17)

After his baptism Jesus emerges from the waters and sees the
Spirit of God descending upon him, but the voice is not for him
alone. It declares who he is: the Son, the Beloved of God, favored by
God. But this voice is also for us. In our baptisms we too become
children of God, brothers and sisters of Jesus. The Holy Spirit
descends on us and we become the Beloved of God! From this
moment on, everything changes at its roots — as was Jesus, we are a
new creation, we are drawn into the kingdom of God on earth, we are
possessed by the favor and power of God. In the rest of the gospel
Jesus lives, breathes, and preaches what it means to relate to God in
this way and what happens when we relate to one another and interpret every event around us through this gift of the Holy Spirit.

Next come Jesus' temptations, but we will deal with them in the
chapter on authority and power. Let us move immediately to Jesus'
first proclamation of the kingdom of God. Once again Matthew,
harkening to the Hebrew Scriptures, repeats Isaiah's prophecy of
the Light that has come into the world, penetrating the darkness of
death (Is 8:23–9:1). Driven by the power of the Spirit, Jesus begins
his preaching: "Repent, for the kingdom of heaven is at hand"
(Mt 4:17). The rest of Matthew's Gospel will dig through the layers
and layers of meaning that the Spirit of God has woven into that one
verse. What follows in chapters 5–7 is the very heart of Jesus' way
of life, God's agenda in the world, what the kingdom is and how it
comes in us and among us — the "Sermon on the Mount." It
includes the Beatitudes, new standards for those who would put the
law into practice; prayer, the heart of which is the Our Father; and
exhortations on money, fasting, almsgiving, and living as true
disciples. This exposition of Jesus' teaching contains the treasure
we seek, the dream of God's kingdom appearing in the world in the
person of Jesus. It is the gift of the very relationship between God
the Father, in the power of the Spirit, with Jesus. It is an attitude of

being, a blessing, an honor and a responsibility. Dig Deeper. The more we read this text, reflect upon it, study it, the more we realize that it is written and shared with us to challenge us, to convert us, to reform and fashion us in the image of the Beloved of God, the children of God's dream on earth, the presence of Jesus that remains always on the earth. We will always find another layer, another level of meaning and wisdom for our lives, alone and together, our way of being holy like Jesus is holy.

The Beatitudes and the Kingdom of Heaven

What is the kingdom of God? This "kingdom" consists not in power and authority but in relationships among the children of God, this new family of Jesus. Matthew's usual phrase, "the kingdom of heaven," suggests the reality that God sees through the veil of the Spirit's truth. This kingdom is realized in those we choose to associate with, to identify and align ourselves with. Those we belong to, those we cast our lot with and share our lives with, those with whom we share our resources and our privilege, our power and freedom. The Beatitudes identify our "kin" in the kingdom, who it is that share with us a relationship with God. In his *The Sermon on the Mount,* Herman Hendrickx reminds us that this family includes all who are "threatened, oppressed, downtrodden," and as their sisters and brothers we must begin to give life to those who have none; to remove all oppressive relationships of one person over another, or nation over another, to bring them to mutual solidarity; to liberate people from any kind of fear; not to condemn people, not to nail them to their sinful past or negative experiences, but to give them in all circumstances a new future, and a hope that brings life; to love people without distinction, without selection, without limits; to oppose what is untrue, what is no longer relevant and has no future, to oppose a legalistic mentality which overlooks the actual person and promotes only uninspired conformity and prayer that is not offered in spirit and truth, but that is mere routine. (2–3)

And that is only the beginning! We must begin with the poor, the marginalized, the outcast, the shunned, those considered expendable. But we must "dig deeper," to those who have done wrong, who disagree with us, who do not "belong" to the groups with which we are comfortable, including our religion. We are bound to those in every nation, religion, race, those relegated to the last caste, the bottom of the heap; those who live on the garbage dumps of the world.

This kingdom of heaven exists wherever God in Jesus acts. This kingdom's power and authority exclude no one, give everyone hope for a reign of justice and peace-making marked by forgiveness, reconciliation, and communion. This kingdom often demands opposition to collusion among institutions of national, governmental, social, economic, and religious power. The kingdom and its people witness against violence, hatred, nationalism, and any evil, oppression, or slavery that robs people of dignity or consigns them to a life of mere subsistence. The community that belongs to this dream-coming-true of the kingdom of heaven reminds itself constantly that it must give public witness of its own need for mutual conversion and transformation at its roots. The baptized are called to live here, with Jesus, as Jesus did in his society and history. We disciples are called to preach and teach this kingdom first to our own cultures and nations, including those in our own church, not with words but with our deeds, our presence, and our obedience to God's vision.

There are other terms for the kingdom of heaven on earth. Martin Luther King, Jr., referred to it as the Beloved Community and he was clear that the Beloved Community was about being and making peace on earth among groups that saw themselves as bitter enemies. He saw his community as God's revolution based on non-violent conflict resolution, restorative justice and peace — beginning with the absence of war, but expanding into a sanctuary and haven, a refuge for the abandoned, the broken, the shunned, and those imprisoned by people in their pasts, their sin, and their slavery.

Jesus commissioned his disciples, once they had become true disciples, converted and transformed into the Word of God, to go into the whole world and make disciples from every nation, baptizing them in the name of the Trinity. They were to teach everything that he had commanded, not with words but by practice, by example, and by their witness. As St. Francis is said to have advised his followers: "Only as a last resort, use words." And so the kingdom of heaven is the mission of Jesus, and our mission on earth.

The Sermon on the Mount (Chapters 4-7)

Jesus starts out blessing those in the kingdom and those invited to accompany them. His words must have floored his listeners because they proclaim loudly God's favor upon masses of people that have no power and no authority in the world. He takes note of eight great groups whom he treats with special regard, even urges his hearers to join! Two groups, the first and last he names, already dwell in the kingdom of heaven now on earth: those who are poor and those who are persecuted for justice's sake. The other six groups are on the way to the kingdom or, having reached it, learning to enter it more deeply. These eight groups are those who are poor, those who are meek (or the gentle, the non-violent), those who mourn, those who are merciful, those who are pure in heart (or single-hearted), those who are peace-makers and those who suffer persecution for the cause of right. Each group is singled out and blessed by Jesus. We usually translate Jesus' words as "blessed are ..." as if those groups are only receiving blessing. The word "blessed" is a translation of the Greek word *makarioi*, but in the Aramaic of Jesus the Beatitudes use *ashray*, from the verb *yashar*. This word has no passive sense at all! In *We Belong to the Land*, Elias Chacour and Mary Evelyn Jensen write that the Aramaic means: "to set yourself on the right way for the right goal; to turn around, repent; to become straight or righteous." They explain the deeper meaning of the Beatitudes using concrete situations in Palestine today:

How could I go to a persecuted young man in a Palestinian refugee camp, for instance, and say, "Blessed are those who mourn, for they shall be comforted," or "Blessed are those who are persecuted for the sake of justice, for theirs is the kingdom of heaven"? That man would revile me, saying neither I nor my God understood his plight, and he would be right. When I understand Jesus' words in the Aramaic, I translate like this: Get up, go ahead, do something, move, you who are hungry and thirsty for justice, for you shall be satisfied. Get up, go ahead, do something, move, you peacemakers, for you shall be called the children of God. To me this reflects Jesus' words and teachings much more accurately. I can hear him saying: "Get your hands dirty to build a human society for human beings; otherwise, others will torture and murder the poor, the voiceless, and the powerless." Christianity is not passive but active, energetic, alive, going beyond despair. "Get up, go ahead, do something, move," Jesus said to his disciples. (143–144)

Entire books have been written about the words and meaning of Jesus' Beatitudes and all his words found in the Sermon on the Mount (see the bibliography for some good ones), yet we can dig deeper still. Or, to put it another way, these words are points of departure for all our behaviors, decisions, choices, priorities, and relationships. They name an attitude of being in the world; they name our agenda, that is, God's agenda, God's dream meant to become reality on earth beginning with the presence of Jesus among us. Without illusion we must begin again and again to clear our eyes and wash out our ears so that we can see and hear, though it stuns us every time, the proclamation of what God intends and expects that we human beings do, with the power of the Spirit, with Jesus, to the glory of the Father on this earth here, now. Each person baptized and confirmed must take personally everything that Jesus says. In the small communities of our local churches and neighborhoods and parishes, and in the grand political bodies of our nations and our churches that stand apart from the powers of the world, we are called to proclaim God's vision of hope and of care for those Jesus names in the Beatitudes. We must make the blessings real. The power of the Word of God works to make this reign, this law, this freedom and truth become real in human society, beginning with the way we live together.

The coming of Jesus has shifted the world's center of gravity toward all the children of God, especially toward those we often refer to as the poor. This is the radical imperative of the gospel, of all of Jesus' words — we are to be the blessing bestowed upon us in Jesus. This is our baptismal commitment, our new life, our New Testament, covenant, and law. And so in light of this shift, we listen to the rest of Jesus' words, letting their import sift through our practices, our relationships, and our choices as individuals and as his community of baptized disciples.

Jesus has given us images to which we are to put flesh and blood and matter — we are to be salt of the earth, the light of the world. We are to build our houses (communities) on solid rock and not on sand. We are not to pray as pagans do, but with trust in the words of Jesus to Our Father. We are to decide who we serve: God or money — which kingdom rules us? What are our priorities in life? Who do we obey when push comes to shove? Why do we care what they think of us? We are to judge carefully, remembering that we will be judged as we have eyed others and pronounced judgment on them. We judge whether others are real prophets or disciples not by their words, "Lord, Lord," but by the fruits of their actions — are they producing good fruit for others or rotten fruit? And we apply the same criteria to ourselves. If we take these words truly to heart we cannot put them into practice alone. Only the community can — these words come to us gathered together to listen to the Word of God in our midst. To live in the kingdom of God as the blessed of God, the beloved children of God, we must belong to others who share the same hope and seek the same treasure. Jesus catches us off guard when he tells us:

> Do not store up for yourselves treasures on earth, where
> moth and decay destroy, and thieves break in and steal. But

store up treasures in heaven, where neither moth nor decay destroys, nor thieves break in and steal. For where your treasure is, there also will your heart be. (Mt 6:19–21)

Where is our treasure? This treasure is not "spiritual or ethereal." It is found in those blessed by God, the children of the Beatitudes, and in our communities that become the blessing of God, the kingdom on earth, a beacon on a hill, communities that to those situations, relationships, and circumstances that need it add infusions of "salt" — flavor, endurance, preservation, healing balm for wounds, even money. And where are our hearts? For Jews in Matthew's day, as it is still for all those in the Mideast today, the heart is not the center of feelings or emotions but the home of the will. Where do we direct our wills? God wants ever more abundant life for all people, but especially those who lack what they need for survival and hope for the future. Is that where we direct our will and resources, work and prayer, where Jesus directed his own words, prayer, life, and hope?

The Spirit's Law

A Hindu story can reveal how to make the Sermon on the Mount and the Beatitudes practical and down to earth. It's called "The Butter in the Milk." It teaches an important lesson for those seeking God and how God operates in their lives, as well as for those seeking to worship God not only in ritual but in their daily lives.

* Once upon a time a girl was searching for God in her life. She decided to go to an elderly saint who lived alone on the edge of the forest and ask where to find God in her life. She found the holy woman sitting in her hut praying. The girl entered, sat before the woman, and waited for her to look up. When she did she bowed forward in respect and asked, "Where can I find God in my life?"

The old woman sat quiet for awhile and then looked up. "That is a hard question, one not easily answered right away. I'd like some time to think about it. Why don't you come back tomorrow around this time and we can talk? Oh, and when you come, please bring me a cup of milk." The girl nodded, rose, and left. She was excited — the woman thought her question important enough to reflect on it. She'd happily bring a cup of milk — the old woman must be thirsty and hungry. With remorse, she realized that she hadn't even thought of bringing a gift in exchange for the old woman's wisdom.

The next day she eagerly sat before the old woman once again and respectfully presented the milk. The old woman poured it into her begging bowl and returned the cup. Then she put her fingers in the bowl and started turning them through the milk, around and around and around, lifting fingers every few minutes and looking at them, her head cocked to one side. Perplexed, the girl watched and wondered what the woman was doing. This went on and on and the girl became impatient — she had come for an answer. What was she doing with the milk? But the old woman didn't even look up. Working with the milk, she stirred it and lifted it, letting it run through her fingers and stirring it again. Unable to bear it any longer the girl finally blurted out: "What are you doing? Are you looking for something? Is there something wrong? The milk is fresh. I know that for sure."

The old woman looked up for a moment and said: "I am looking for the butter in the milk. I have been told that there is butter in milk, but I can't seem to find it. I have been looking very hard for it in this milk."

Without realizing it, the young woman laughed at her and said: "That's not the way it is! There is butter in the milk but it's not separate from the milk. You have to work at it — you have to convert the milk into yogurt first and then churn it before the butter comes out!" As she finished speaking she realized the old woman most certainly already knew this — and she stopped, thinking about her own words. This process of finding butter in the milk — was it like finding God in your own life?

The old woman smiled at her. "Ah, you're learning. The wisdom of the milk and your own life is surfacing to teach you.

"If you go home and reflect on this — and it might help to make a lot of yogurt and butter for others in the process — you will find the answer to your question. God is already there in your life — and everywhere. There is nowhere that God is not, but you have to churn the milk of your heart and soul and life to find God there." And with that, the old woman drank the cup of milk and thanked the girl for the gift and they both smiled.

It's all in the milk! Wisdom and answers are found in the gift that you give to another. What another drinks saves you. In others' needs, in hospitality, every place you may not be aware — especially there you find God. But it is work, the work of a lifetime, and best done together with others.

In this opening sermon Jesus calls his disciples to churn through their lives, their society, their souls to find God there — everywhere, and to look in places that society, nation, and religion may have ignored, even condemned. The presence of God in Jesus opens up possibilities in the most unlikely places — even in milk, yogurt, butter, ice cream! Where are we looking? What in our world are we churning and making into food, making it richer and more available to others? Jesus tells his disciples to start churning within society, but also to be mindful of the law — to dig deeper and deeper for its wisdom so that they might know how to obey the law and God, as Jesus obeys God, our Father.

Beginning with the Torah, the Law of Moses and the prophets, Jesus says what we must do to understand true obedience. We must take the law to heart, read the rest of what he has to say about it, and look at how he practices it as well as how he breaks it:

> Do not think that I have come to abolish the law or the prophets. I have come not to abolish but to fulfill. Amen, I say to you, until heaven and earth pass away, not the smallest letter or the smallest part of a letter will pass from the law, until all things have taken place. Therefore, whoever breaks one of the least of these commandments and teaches others to do so will be called least in the kingdom of heaven. But whoever obeys and teaches these

commandments will be called greatest in the kingdom of heaven. I tell you, unless your righteousness surpasses that of the scribes and Pharisees, you will not enter into the kingdom of heaven. (Mt 5:17–20)

This is not what we might expect. Jesus tells us first to honor and respect the law, to know it intimately and obey it. But then he tells us that we must go beyond the usual interpretations and practice — we must go deeper and deeper into the law to know it inside out, from God's point of view. And then Jesus proceeds to interpret the most basic laws beginning with the injunction against the first sin of the human race — murder: You must not kill! Obviously we must not kill any other human being, but that is not enough — we must not hate, bear resentment, rage, act in anger against another. We must not insult or humiliate others. And this extends to worship. We must not appear before God severed from anyone, ready to kill anyone or harm another, even thinking of revenge or getting even with others. We will be judged by how we practice the law with all our heart (will), mind, soul, resources, even with our intent and thoughts. This is the corner we must learn to turn with every law.

Jesus continues with the law: "You have heard that it was said, 'You shall not commit adultery.' But I say to you, everyone who looks at a woman with lust has already committed adultery with her in his heart" (Mt 5:19–20). Not only is the physical act of adultery — sexual relations with someone other than one's wife or husband — wrong. Much more transpires before the action itself is performed. We are just as culpable for what goes on in our minds, our hearts, and our intentions as we are for the actual deed of adultery. And the law extends to men and women alike — it is the same for all.

Jesus next cites the law concerning swearing oaths: "Do not take a false oath, but make good to the Lord all that you vow." Oaths sworn to others are secondary, not to be confused with oaths made to God. Our language is to be clear: Yes or No, without adding language such as "by God" that use God as backup to mere human words.

The next command, an ancient one, is still used today, but in its earlier version and out of context from anything that Jesus says is true:

> You have heard that it was said: "An eye for an eye and a
> tooth for a tooth." But I say to you, offer no resistance to
> one who is evil. When someone strikes you on (your) right
> cheek, turn the other one to him as well. If anyone wants to
> go to law with you over your tunic, hand him your cloak as
> well. Should anyone press you into service for one mile,
> go with him for two miles. Give to the one who asks of you
> and do not turn your back on one who wants to borrow.
> (Mt 5:38–42)

Imagine the response of Jesus' disciples and the crowd as these words
build up and build up shattering all the usual ways of looking at and
obeying the law. Hearing how God intends that we live with one
another on the earth, they would have murmured, then fallen speechless, dumbfounded, stunned. This is revolutionary. This demands far
more than anything the prophets preached. This teaching "astonished
them, for he taught them as one having authority, and not as their
scribes" (Mt 7:29). And how do we react to these words? With outright
resistance, disbelief, rejection of Jesus' words and their deeper intent?

Jesus cites one more specific example from the law: "You must
love your neighbor and hate your enemy." The notes in the Jerusalem
Bible explain that in the original Aramaic the second part of this
commandment ("hate your enemy") "is equivalent to 'There is less
obligation to love one's enemy' " (note *n*, Mt 5:43):

> But I say to you, love your enemies, and pray for those
> who persecute you, that you may be children of your heav-
> enly Father, for he makes his sun rise on the bad and the
> good, and causes rain to fall on the just and the unjust. For
> if you love those who love you, what recompense will you
> have? Do not the tax collectors do the same? And if you
> greet your brothers only, what is unusual about that? Do
> not the pagans do the same? So be perfect, just as your
> heavenly Father is perfect. (Mt 5:43–48)

We must remember that this is Jesus' first sermon, exhorting us,
pointing us in the right direction. That does not mean that it is only an
ideal — no, Jesus' words and practice presume a community, a body

that has been baptized and formed in church, the household of God, the kingdom people on earth. And it matters not if we argue about whether it is to be taken literally — it is to be taken layer upon layer, ever deeper, encompassing more of our lives with each reading and each day. This is how we are to live now with the presence of the risen Jesus among us. The law as Jesus interprets it is a survival manual of skills and insights on how to live in a world hostile to love, to forgiveness and reconciliation, to peacemaking, to a community that refuses to be violent. These words are meant to be followed, practiced, and lived with imagination and creativity. Jesus expects us to live according to this new order of creation, this way, his way of the truth and life and light. God expects us to live in peace. We must remember that Jesus' very being, his every action and word is in God's presence, is the Light in the world. In his book on the Sermon on the Mount, *Into the Darkness,* Gene Davenport writes:

> When the first hearers of Matthew's Gospel heard Jesus'
> call to suffer rather than to inflict suffering, to accept
> death rather than to inflict death, to reject all efforts to
> save themselves from their plight by military action and to
> leave their deliverance to God, they knew that the one who
> gave such scandalous instruction had himself lived and
> died in accord with that call. (15)

We cannot do this as isolated individuals. To live single-heartedly and faithfully in all our relationships, to marry without divorce, to refuse taking oaths, to refuse returning evil and hatred in retaliation and to love our enemies and give to all who beg from us, we must act with the heart and soul and support of a community. We build our houses on rock together or we slide along with the sand into the sea alone. These words of Jesus introduce us to the kingdom of heaven on earth in his presence, open the gates and invite us in. Describing this marvelous reality, Thomas Merton writes:

> The great historical event, the coming of the Kingdom,
> is made clear and is "realized" in proportion as Chris-
> tians themselves live the life of the Kingdom in the
> circumstances of their own place and time. The saving

grace of God in the Lord Jesus is proclaimed to man existentially in the love, the openness, the simplicity, the humility and the self-sacrifice of Christians.... The religious basis of Christian nonviolence is, then, faith in Christ the Redeemer and obedience to his demand to love and manifest himself in us by a certain manner of acting in the world and in relation to other men. This obedience enables us to live as true citizens of the kingdom, in which the divine mercy, the grace, favor and redeeming love of God are active in our lives. Then the Holy Spirit will indeed "rest upon us" and act in us, not for our own good alone but for God and his kingdom. (18–22)

This sermon of Jesus, grounded in the power and authority that is his from the Father, grounds all that will follow. Jesus' summary law is simple: "So be perfect just as your heavenly Father is perfect" (Mt 5:48). Now it is time to look to the Father of Jesus revealed in Jesus by the power of the Spirit as the source of Jesus' graceful life and our own lives as God's beloved children.

Questions

1. What is your reaction to Jesus' extending the law into the realm of spirit, intent, thought, and practice toward everyone?

2. Which particular saying of Jesus found in the Sermon on the Mount do you resist most? Why?

3. Which of the groups of those who are blessed do you have the most difficulty with — why? What is your experience of these people? Where do you find them today in the world?

4. Who is your community — the people who share belief in Jesus with you, study the scriptures with you each week, and hold you accountable for continual conversion? What is it like to hold another accountable for change? And what does your community think you need to be held accountable for most often?

4
Our Father: The Authority and Power of Jesus

There is a marvelous children's story from Southeast Asia called "In the Middle." It is for four-year-olds and up, so I suspect that would include most of us. This is the way I tell it:

* Once upon a time a young father took his son to sell their produce in the next village. It had been a good day and after selling all they had brought they wandered around. The father took delight in showing his son everything and answering his questions. Before they realized it, it had grown very late. They headed home, following the path into the jungle. The young father didn't want to worry his son, but he himself was concerned that they were heading home so late. And walking at the pace of a tired child, he realized they would have to stay overnight in the jungle.

When the boy was exhausted, the father found a spot under a great palm tree by the river, and cleared an area for the two of them. He lay down on the palm fronds and patted the ground beside him, telling his child to lie down and sleep with him. The boy was afraid, for it grew dark quickly and unfamiliar sounds filled the night. The boy moved toward his father but began to say over and over again. "I want the middle! Let me sleep in the middle!" The father had no idea what he was talking about — the middle of what? The middle of where?

69

But the boy would not be comforted or put off — "I want the middle! I want to sleep in the middle!" Finally the boy pushed his father down on his back and crawled in between his father's legs, resting his chest and head on his father's stomach under his chin. "Ah," he said, "the middle." His father smiled. It was a good place for the child to sleep. And though there were many noises, they eventually both fell asleep, tired from the day's outing.

In the middle of the night a tiger coming down to the river to drink smelled humans. He padded around sniffing everywhere, and came upon the man and his child. But what was this thing? In the dusky light it appeared to have four legs and four arms and two heads. This was new to the tiger. He came closer and smelled up and down the legs and arms and torso and then came to the father's head. He sniffed his hair and cheeks. The great whiskers tickling the man's skin make him awake with a loud sneeze: *Achoo!* Both he and the young boy sat up alarmed and the tiger jumped back in surprise, then bolted! As the man hugged his child and rocked him back to sleep, the boy hummed silently: "In the middle. I sleep in the middle." The tiger had terrified the man, but he knew it would not return, it had been so startled. When morning came, they resumed their journey home. The boy was laughing, darting in and out, discovering everything and asking questions.

When they arrived home, all the boy spoke about was the trip. His mother, concerned about where they had slept, was startled to hear her child say: "It was the best sleep. I was in the middle. I slept in the middle." At the explanation of what "the middle" was, she smiled. The child had been safe, and secure "in the middle" of his father.

When I told this story of a father and son to children in Southeast Asia, they responded: "And we, we are the beloved children of God." And in Jesus' Spirit, we are always "in the middle" of our Father.

Our Father, the Father of Jesus shared with us in the Spirit of Jesus is the source and root of Jesus' power and authority on earth.

We will look at this power and authority, how Jesus prays to his Father, and what Jesus' sharing that relationship with us means for our lives as believers.

The Testing of Jesus

Matthew places the story of Jesus being tested in the desert prior to his public preaching of the kingdom of heaven as a signpost, to warn us that we too will be tempted to diverge from the kingdom and to attempt bringing God's kingdom into the world by means other than those Jesus knows are the only ones born of God's will, but also to give us hope. Will we stand the test as Jesus did? The story also highlights the tension that fills much of Matthew's Gospel: struggle with groups that resist Jesus; with religious authorities threatened by his power, words, and authority with the people; and conflict that Jesus himself experiences with his own disciples and loved ones. He must constantly return to his own soul and the Spirit within him to remain true to who he is as the Beloved Child of God.

The order of the tests is significant. The first and the second begin with the words: "If you are the Son of God, then …" Satan (the word means hinderer, or accuser) is trying to find out who Jesus is, just as the tests we undergo in our lives reveal to us and others who we really are. Many will seek to hinder Jesus from bringing the kingdom of heaven among us and he will face much resistance to his words, his work and his very person. Matthew is interested in linking Jesus to the Jews ancestors in the desert, during the Exodus. Just as God called his son out of Egypt earlier, now along with the people of God, Jesus will sojourn in the desert as they did, but much more intensely:

> Remember how for forty years now the Lord, your God, has directed all your journeying in the desert, so as to test you by affliction and find out whether or not it was your intention to keep his commandments. He therefore let you be afflicted with hunger, and then fed you with manna, a

> food unknown to you and your fathers, in order to show you that not by bread alone does man live, but by every word that comes forth from the mouth of the Lord.... So you must realize that the Lord, your God, disciplines you even as a man disciplines his son. (Dt 8:2–5)

This passage from Deuteronomy provides the backdrop for Jesus' test. It is significant that each time Jesus is tested, he responds by quoting scripture — the Word of God. As did Jesus, in the Word of God, in the scriptures, we too find the response we need and suggestions for resolving our conflicts and trials. Instead of forty years (a lifetime or a generation) Jesus' trial of forty days represents what will happen to each of us over an entire lifetime.

The first test is connected to basic survival: "If you are the Son of God, command that these stones become loaves of bread." Jesus replies: "It is written: 'One does not live by bread alone, but by every word that comes forth from the mouth of God' " (Mt 4:3–4). Jesus is hungry, but his manna in the desert is the Word of God. This is our food for the journey, sustenance for body and soul, if we are to survive as beloved children of our Father. God alone can satisfy the hunger of every human being and of humankind. This passage makes us consider whom we trust and whom we rely on — the true source of our security, beginning with our work and our basic human needs: food, clothing, water, shelter, medicine, health care, education, dignity. As sons and daughters of God, no matter our circumstances, no matter our wealth or poverty, we are to dwell in community and share what is given to all among all, as over their long process of becoming his, God removed the people from slavery in Egypt and fed them in the desert.

The second test takes Jesus higher — both literally, when he is taken to the holy city and placed upon the highest point of the Temple, its parapet, and figuratively, into the realm of religious belief, into the institutions of faith. "If you are the Son of God, throw yourself down. For it is written: 'He will command his angels concerning you,' and 'with their hands they will support you, lest you dash your foot against a stone' " (Mt 4:5–6).

The hinderer uses Jesus' own tactic of quoting scripture to get Jesus to do what Satan wants rather than what God wants. But Jesus is quick to retort: "Again it is written: 'You shall not put the Lord, your God, to the test.' " His words recall what happened in the wilderness when the people sought to put God to the test. They were thirsty and complained to Moses that God had brought them out to kill them and their children and livestock (see Ex 17:3). Not trusting what God had told him to do, to satisfy them, Moses strikes the rock twice. When things got rough the people whined, "Is the Lord in our midst or not?" (Ex 17:7). Jesus is clear that he trusts God and will not test God by demanding that God save him from harm, protect him from evil, or perform a miracle to save him. And he is not going to insult the Lord of Hosts with a demand for acknowledgment that he is loved and held in God's providence by foolishly jumping off the Temple.

The last test is on a high mountain, echoing God taking Moses, before he dies, up Mount Nebo to show him the promised land before the people enter (see Dt 34:1–4). Moses is shown what God will give him and the people; Satan shows Jesus what he'll give him. In the mouth of Satan the words of this last test are chilling:

> Then the devil took him up to a very high mountain, and showed him all the kingdoms of the world in their magnificence, and he said to him, "All these I shall give to you, if you will prostrate yourself and worship me." At this, Jesus said to him, "Get away, Satan! It is written: 'The Lord, your God, shall you worship and him alone shall you serve.' "
> (Mt 4:8–10)

With the covenant God gives and gives and gives and asks worship in return. Satan as well gives what is of the world and wants worship in return. You cannot have it both ways. The hinderer wants Jesus' allegiance, his soul, and his life in Satan's service, using the Satanic forms of power and authority: war, murder, hatred, nationalism, poverty, slavery, inequality, selfishness, destruction of the earth and abuse of resources, knowledge, and power. Like Jesus we will face a lifetime of choices. In his first sermon Jesus puts it bluntly: "No one can serve two masters. He will either hate one and love the other, or be devoted to one and despise the other. You cannot serve God and mammon" (Mt 6:24).

Like Jesus, we need certain things to survive, but no need is greater than our relationship to God based on trust and obedience, not miracles, and our need to know that God is with us and to live life based on that belief, not to be seduced by the world's power and authority. We either live as children of the kingdom of God, visionaries of God's dream and revolutionaries of God's utter peacefulness, or we play the power games of earth's power bases. We must choose. Jesus chooses — God alone will he serve and obey; to God alone does he belong. We must choose. And when we do, we are drawn ever deeper into Jesus' relationship with the Father in the power of the Spirit.

Prayer as Jesus Prays

Hebrew and Aramaic as well as Greek offer this remarkable definition of prayer: "to stand in the presence of God, to be seen for who you are and not to run away." Jesus says much about prayer, especially prayer to our Father in heaven, and he himself prays, sometimes aloud, and often in silence, hidden from others. We too are to learn this pattern. Even in his first sermon Jesus tells us repeatedly that our Father sees and knows what we do, what we need, how we pray, and how we give alms. And we are not to pray like pagans who do not know their God. We are to pray in public, but we are also to pray and fast and give alms in secret. In all we do, we are to take as our criterion, our model, the perfection, the holiness, and the compassion of our Father God.

And the first prayer we are given to pray in public, aloud and with one another, is the Lord's Prayer. Before we even begin we are to remember that our Father knows what we need — we do not have to ask. When we pray like Jesus, we pray about what God the Father would like from us, not what we would like from God. Such prayer is about reminding ourselves of God's kingdom, God's will, and God's favor with us and all peoples. There are many translations of the Our Father, but it covers just seven requests. Three have to do with God's kingdom of heaven and four have to do with all of us, God's children in that kingdom. We are first to bless God's name, bring God's kingdom, and do God's will on earth as it is in heaven. And then we are to look to ourselves to see if we are living that kingdom in our lives now. We ask for bread, only what we (all of us on earth) need today. We ask forgiveness for our debts (not for our sins) in the measure that we forgive those who are in debt to us. We ask that we will survive and pass through the tests of our lives and that at the end we will be saved.

It is stunningly simple, direct, to the point, and devastating, since most of our prayers are totally disconnected from anything in this prayer. Or worse we rattle senselessly through the Our Father, the Lord's Prayer, unaware or unconscious of what we, all of us together, are praying with Jesus in the power of the Spirit of God. This praying puts us in the presence of God, like Moses on holy ground, but even more so with Jesus who comes with us, prays with us and the Spirit that prays within us. The preface for the 8th Sunday of Ordinary Time says: "Father, may you see and love in us what you saw and loved in Jesus!" This is praying the Lord's praying. This is the source and root of Jesus' power and authority in all that he does and says on earth. And the tag at the end of the Lord's Prayer reads:

> If you forgive others their transgressions, your heavenly Father will forgive you. But if you do not forgive others, neither will your Father forgive your transgressions. (Mt 6:14)

We cannot sever our words from our deeds, our forgiveness of others, and how we dwell in community and relate to others in the world.[1]

---

1. A later chapter discusses this imperative to forgive, forgiveness as a way of life expressing our worship and belief in God our Father and as the foundation of community in God.

In the paragraphs that follow, Jesus reminds us gently to look at the birds of the sky and the flowers of the field and not to worry about how we are to live and what we are to wear, and eat, or about collecting possessions. Our prayer must mirror our trust in God who sees and knows our needs and provides for everyone and everything in creation. We are to be different than pagans — those who run after material things. Again Jesus reminds us:

> Your heavenly Father knows that you need them all. But seek first the kingdom (of God) and his righteousness, and all these things will be given you besides. (Mt 6:33)

We must not worry or spend our energies and time self-absorbed and fretting about every little thing. We are worth more than sparrows and crows and ravens, more than any flower or weed. How we work and what we do with our money and time must reflect our faith. We are to ask, to seek and search and to knock at the door. It will be given to us — it may not be precisely what we asked for, but we will receive what God knows we need. In our prayers we must dare and risk, trusting that all that our God gives us is good, as God fathers us and sustains us and makes us mature adult children like Jesus. At the deepest part of our lives, our souls, and our prayer must lie the kingdom of heaven, God's dream of justice and peace for all. And we must ask, seek, and knock on behalf of all that need it now. We must remember that when Jesus speaks of the kingdom of heaven it is *never* about a kingdom in another world or time. It is always right here on earth, right now. We must make sure that our prayers address the heart of the matter and not remain superficial. We are here, with Jesus, to complete the kingdom that he has brought into the world with his presence. We must be about the sharing of bread, about forgiving together the debts we are owed, and about redeeming the world, everything and everyone in it. All that Jesus does is about feeding, preaching, teaching, and healing. These tasks are our priorities too. The Our Father is communal prayer about peace-making with an unmistakably public, political, and economic tone. Speaking the word Abbuni — Our Father — aloud testifies and witnesses to our faith in communion with Jesus. That spoken name is the source of our strength, our enduring grace, our power and authority.

Jesus' Authority

Jesus teaches and preaches with power. With authority, he touches those who are abused, excluded, shunned, and condemned. His very presence exudes an authority and power that draws the people like a magnet. Much later in the gospel (chapter 21) he drives the money changers out of the Temple, accepts the praise of the people as he enters Jerusalem on a donkey, and curses a barren fig tree because it bears no fruit (an image of many leaders in the community). Some, however, question his authority outright or intrigue against him, a game that will eventually turn deadly:

> When he had come into the temple area, the chief priests and the elders of the people approached him as he was teaching and said, "By what authority are you doing these things? And who gave you this authority?" Jesus said to them in reply, "I shall ask you one question, and if you answer it for me, then I shall tell you by what authority I do these things. Where was John's baptism from? Was it of heavenly or of human origin?" They discussed this among themselves and said, "If we say 'Of heavenly origin,' he will say to us, 'Then why did you not believe him?' But if we say, 'Of human origin,' we fear the crowd, for they all regard John as a prophet." So they said to Jesus in reply, "We do not know." He himself said to them, "Neither shall I tell you by what authority I do these things." (Mt 21:23–27)

From the beginning, Jesus' public preaching and teaching infuriates the leaders of the people: the scribes and the chief priests. They are rankled by his attitude toward people considered sinners, unclean or unsaved, and by what they consider his violating the law, disregarding it, or deepening its requirements. He is infringing on their territory and invading their domain, their kingdoms of control and power over the people. Their animus toward Jesus grows and heightens from anger into rage and then into hatred. They are not interested in being truthful, in dialogue or discussion — they want to trap him in their games of deceit and their manipulation of the law and their traditions so as to find an excuse to destroy him. Jesus' power is born of truth, embedded in God as Father and in the Spirit of God that is layered through the Word of God, through the Torah of the Law and the Prophets. The Law and the Prophets (every word that comes forth from the mouth of God) is gift and covenant, meant to convert and transform the people. Sadly, these people, the scribes and chief priests, are not interested in conversion. They are intent on retaining their public position of power, so they consider Jesus a threat. And so Jesus is hard in his response to them. He will not play their game.

He continues with a parable meant to shove right in their faces the truth of their hatred and their resistance to his words. They know that the scriptures call the people of God, Israel, the "Son of God," yet here in the Temple courtyard they are divided and fighting, their ears closed to God's Word. Jesus goes after them head-on:

> What is your opinion? A man had two sons. He came to the first and said, "Son, go out and work in the vineyard today." He said in reply, "I will not," but afterwards he changed his mind and went. The man came to the other son and gave the same order. He said in reply, "Yes, sir," but did not go. Which of the two did his father's will?
>
> They answered, "The first." Jesus said to them, "Amen, I say to you, tax collectors and prostitutes are entering the kingdom of God before you. When John came to you in the way of righteousness, you did not believe him; but tax collectors and prostitutes did. Yet even when you saw that, you did not later change your minds and believe in him." (Mt 21:25–32)

Jesus continues with other parables but they are a bit thick and slow. Nevertheless, they eventually realize that he is speaking about them, condemning them in their own terms. In reaction they resist more and more stubbornly and turn on him more and more in their hearts. At the end of this chapter we read: "When the chief priests and the Pharisees heard his parables, they knew that he was speaking about them. And although they were attempting to arrest him, they feared the crowds, for the people regarded him as a prophet" (Mt 21:45–46). They do not see Jesus as a prophet — one who bears the Word of God in his mouth and speaks truly, threatening the leaders with what will happen if they do not change yet offering hope if they do repent. They see him as someone to be eliminated and disposed of — no matter how violently.

Jesus tells them the truth. Those they despise — tax collectors who colluded with the Romans to profit from their own people's misery and prostitutes who were abhorrent because of their connection to the fertility gods and goddesses of other religions — are already in the kingdom before them! These public sinners whom the religious leadership humiliated had seen and heard the truth of John's preaching and were baptized and changed, while the leaders themselves, seeing John as a meddlesome threat to their own collusion with the Roman authorities and to their barricaded lives, refused to listen. They wouldn't even entertain the reality that they too were sinners, doing the same sins they accused the detested tax collectors and prostitutes of doing. They certainly weren't cut to the quick of their hearts and repenting. They are the ones who say what is expected but refuse to go and work in the vineyard (again the image of Israel — the covenanted people of God). The people are saying yes to the kingdom of heaven but the leaders, enmeshed in their own twisted positions of power, prestige, and honor, are saying no.

There are many different kinds of power and authority. Some of the more obvious include: the authority of military might; the authority of economic power; the authority of nationalism; the authority of tyrannical government; the authority of elected government; the authority of culture and tradition; the authority of knowledge, skill, or expertise; the authority of age and experience; the authority of the dominant thought, religion, and culture; the authority of institutions; the authority of ordained or self-appointed ministry; the authority of appointment in the academy, philanthropic organizations, corporations, or government; the authority of abuse, or of threat and manipulation through fear and insecurity; the authority of physical force. When the leaders demand that Jesus tell them by what authority he operates, they are thinking in terms of these kinds of power and authority — they do not see that Jesus' authority and power bears no resemblance to any forms of worldly power.

Jesus' power and authority are rooted in the kingdom of heaven and in God his Father and our Father, and the Spirit of Word and Truth. That kingdom has other forms of power and authority — the power and authority of forgiveness, reconciliation, and restoration; the authority of restorative justice; the authority of mercy unbounded; the authority of love, even love unto death; the authority of service and humility; the authority that heals and gives hope; the authority of self-sacrifice and sharing even with extreme generosity; the authority of communal practice of virtue in prayer, fasting, almsgiving, and solidarity with others; the authority of nonviolence; the authority of truth-telling, peace-making and seeking justice by being a voice on behalf of others in need; the authority of witness and martyrdom by laying down one's life on a daily basis in the proclamation of truth, but also by giving one's own life as the last word and testimony. These are some of the powers and authorities of the Spirit, all of which provide the source of Jesus' prayer, words, deeds, and very presence.

Matthew's Gospel is sprinkled with references to why we are to live in obedience to the words of Jesus, whom we serve and worship, and to what constitutes the heart of each of our relationships with God the Father, with Jesus, in the power of the Spirit, because of our baptisms. Because of these references that keep returning to Jesus' words at moments of insight, prayer, and preaching, Matthew's Gospel in many ways can be called the Gospel of the Father. The first reference appears in the middle of the Sermon on the Mount: "Your light must shine before others, that they may see your good deeds and glorify your heavenly Father" (Mt 5:16). This segment of Jesus' preaching culminates in the exhortation that we are all to "be perfect just as your heavenly Father is perfect." We are to be holy as the Father is holy. We are to be compassionate as the Father is compassionate. We are to be filled with tender regard for all as the Father is filled with tender regard for all

— statements of astonishing power and demands. Before the first sermon concludes, Jesus reminds his listeners again that our Father knows what everything needs, from the sparrows and flowers, even the weeds of the field, to every human being. Our Father knows what we need for survival and what we long for. Our Father knows!

Jesus will return again and again to his own relation to the Father as the first gift of the kingdom of heaven on earth, shared with each of the baptized, and that this relation is to grow and mature with discipleship and obedience to Jesus' Word. In his sermon instructing those who follow him to remain steadfast in the midst of persecution, torture, arrest, and betrayal he stands with them, assuring them and us: "Everyone who acknowledges me before others I will acknowledge before my heavenly Father. But whoever denies me before others, I will deny before my heavenly Father" (Mt 10:32–33).

Knowing and Being Known by the Father

Jesus is the power and authority of God enfleshed fully in a human being. The mystery of the Incarnation is God made human, the Word spoken in flesh and blood and bone in Jesus. This is in itself the Good News: the Gospel of God that is "close at hand" in the person of Jesus. When he is being rejected by his own people and misunderstood by his disciples, Jesus speaks of this intimate and singular relationship that he knows with the Father in the power of the Spirit. He laments that so few actually see him for who he is and realize what he is trying to give them — the Father and the kingdom of heaven:

> At that time Jesus said in reply, "I give praise to you, Father, lord of heaven and earth, for although you have hidden these things from the wise and the learned you have revealed them to the childlike. Yes, Father, such has been your gracious will. All things have been handed over to me by my Father. No one knows the Son except the Father, and no one knows the Father except the Son and anyone to whom the Son wishes to reveal him." (Mt 11:25–27)

This simple paragraph speaks in layers of mystery and knowledge of God, of how Jesus and the Father relate to one another and how each is known by the other, and who this knowledge can be shared with as gift from the beloved Son. The opening address echoes the Lord's Prayer but blesses the Father for hiding his identity from those who think they can learn it by their own doing or skill. The mystery and intimacy of how God is in the Father and the Son is revealed to "the childlike." It is crucial to remember that this has nothing to do with age or the emotional and psychological traits that we assign to children (from birth to about 15 years old). At the time of Jesus, children in the Middle Eastern world had no rights and no power — no authority, not even to exist. They survive at the whim and mercy of adults and must obey everyone older or physically stronger — not only relatives and neighbors, but strangers and enemies as well. Children were in the same category as slaves, servants, the sick, the sinner, the outcast, the shunned, the gentile, and the infirm. That is what makes this assertion so shocking. Yet, this is the image that Jesus will use to speak to his disciples of the true disciple, the truly obedient one among them — the humble, the servant of all, the least of the community.

God does not hide any of his wisdom and knowledge — even of who he is and who Jesus is — from the child, the beloved child of God like Jesus. Only the Father knows the Son and the Son has been entrusted with everything by the Father. God shares everything with Jesus — the completeness of his identity, power, and authority — and that is his gift to share with others. No one knows the Father except the Son, and anyone Jesus chooses to share that revelation with! And it is among mere children that this knowledge is shared best, in community! The community of God's children, the brothers and sisters of Jesus, the least in the kingdom, is the privileged place of revelation. Who are these children? We know that — the children of the Beatitudes and those who serve them and seek God's complete goodness, justice, and peace on behalf of them: those who are to be disciples and witnesses with Jesus in the world.

Jesus is weary, down-hearted, discouraged, even lamenting that so many are rejecting him, ignoring him and his words, not to mention those who are seeking more and more actively to stop him from preaching this message of hope and healing and closeness to God in one another, in body and in soul. He continues his own prayer to the Father aloud so that those who are listening to him can take heart from him:

> Come to me, all you who labor and are burdened, and I will give you rest. Take my yoke upon you and learn from me, for I am meek and humble of heart; and you will find rest for yourselves. For my yoke is easy, and my burden light. (Mt 11:28–30)

This prayer is a command — *Come!* — as well as an invitation to all those who labor in the kingdom of heaven and feel overwhelmed, burdened, and discouraged that nothing seems to change, nothing is happening; that all their work is coming to naught, or they are ignored or rejected, even shunned, thought fools, or given a hard time (let alone truly persecuted) for justice's sake. When we are thoroughly exhausted from the work of the kingdom (and it is work) we are invited to draw more closely to the presence and person of Jesus and we will be given rest, solace, comfort, refuge, relief — the same that Jesus knows in his relation to the Father. The prayer is directed at those crushed by the responsibilities and the daily work of the kingdom — providing for others, working in the vineyard (feeding and giving drink to others); making the world holy and transforming every aspect of life and creation, resisting evil, violence, and injustice; serving the poor and abused — all the images of the Good Shepherd who pastures, waters, spreads a table for the flock, feeds, protects, and gives rest to his own. These duties are not primarily liturgical or religious, but the burden of the work of the kingdom on earth that all must assume.

But Jesus also issues a second command: "Take my yoke upon you and learn from me." The yoke is a three-fold symbol. It was used to hold two work animals together so that they could do more work than either could do alone — usually plowing a field (planting the seed of the Word), circling a well to draw forth water (bringing the waters of baptism), threshing grain on a floor (making manna that feeds both body and soul in the kingdom here on earth), or carrying large burdens (both products and people). An older animal was often yoked with a younger one so that the younger would learn steadfastness and discipline and the older would not have to carry the weight alone. We are told to lean together into the work, our tasks, and walk with Jesus who in the Incarnation was yoked to the human race in body and soul.

The yoke also recalls an image of slaves and those condemned to death: yoked to a bar they carried huge loads, burdened with the work of building, transporting, and walking long distances — just as Israel lived in Egypt. Jesus also was yoked to the cross, which he carried length-wise, tied across his shoulders. The upright piece of the cross remained planted in the ground of the garbage dump outside Jerusalem where the executions took place, but the condemned person carried his own instrument of torture and death with him through the city streets. "Take up your yoke" is another way of saying: pick up your cross and come after me. Bear your share of the burden of the gospel and bear one another's burdens as I bear your burden.

And the final image is that of dancing! In the film *Zorba the Greek*, Zorba has lost everything — as he says "the full catastrophe!" And yet he grabs his English friend and shows him how to dance. He throws an arm over his friend's shoulder and together with the workers they all lock arms shoulder to shoulder and they slowly begin the steps of the dance then, as the beat of the music picks up, they dance furiously, ecstatically until they are spent and collapse laughing, having lost everything but the precious gift and burden of life itself. We must take up the yoke of Jesus: in our work, in our attitudes and responses toward others, and in our pain and suffering, even death for the glory of the Father and the kingdom of heaven that is coming upon the earth. And we too will join in the dance of resurrection!

And when we have shouldered his burden as our own, where does the strength and rest that Jesus will share with us come from? It comes from gentleness and humility of heart. A person with gentleness is mild, nonviolent, meek (one of the Beatitudes), and humble

— living close to the earth and its poorest and least, and knowing one's rightful place in the world and before God. This is the power and authority that Jesus is graciously willing to share with us, in prayer, in silence, in presence, and in our need and yearning.

Jesus' prayer, "Come to me, all you who labor and are burdened ..." is as complete and deep as the prayer of the Our Father. We are allowed to overhear Jesus' prayer to the Father and are invited into it, to share his own intimacy and knowledge. Later chapters of Matthew's Gospel contain more allusions and direct references to the Father, but we must always return to these foundational pieces and learn to treasure and practice them, not only in our own individual relation to God, but together as Jesus' brothers and sisters in the power of the Spirit before the Father. Jesus presents this prayer and the Lord's Prayer not only for his followers (though perhaps especially for them) but also for those broken in body and spirit, the defeated, those who stand in solidarity with the world's poorest and the least. It is for all who feel desperate because they are losing hope, losing the ground they stand on, losing their own sense of power, self-worth, and dignity, all who feel vulnerable yet open to repentance, redirection, and transformation. It is for those all too aware of their own sin, shortcomings, insecurities, and failures, all too aware of how their own deficiencies have affected others — or infected others with despair and loneliness. Jesus cries out: "Come to me!" His prayer is evangelization — preaching the gospel. "Come to me. Repent. And believe in the kingdom of heaven that is close at hand!" — close at hand in Jesus and in every human being, as close as the person nearest to us. Here, Jesus prays for community — for making community and for making people aware of their profound need for community in God. He prays to remind the world that we are all one in God and that our relation to God is only as close as our relation to others — that we are yoked to the cross and to one another, that we are made in the sign of the Cross.

But he also wants us to dance together, yoked in the freedom of the children of God, supporting one another, sharing each others' precious burdens here in the kingdom, teaching each other how to make our lives "easy and light."

Questions

1. When you pray to Jesus' Father as "Our Father" who do you include in your prayer and life when you say "our"?

2. Are you "yoked together" with anyone in the sense of sharing with another person, or a few people, the work and the ministry of bringing the Father's kingdom to earth? How do you help one another? How do you hinder one another?

3. What power of the kingdoms of the world do you follow and fear? Why do you fear it? What power do you want to have? Why?

4. Who in your community models one of the powers or authority that Jesus practices — based on his or her relationship to the Father, with Jesus, in the power of the Spirit? What would it be like to ask that person (or those persons) to teach you and share that power with you — as Jesus seeks to share his power with us?

5

Forgiveness: The Deepest Treasure of the Kingdom

The kingdom of heaven among us is Jesus, the Word made flesh, his presence and his Word. This is the first treasure we find, the first dream of God for the human community. But we can find other treasures only when we dig deeper and are open to sharing what we have been given with others — strangers, beggars, or even those we call enemies. We rarely find this deeper treasure in individuals, but we always find it in community. It is the source of community, what sustains, renews and repairs. It is the gift of forgiveness. Jesus is the forgiveness of God. In Jesus all of humanity is forgiven, made whole, and reunited with God — in Jesus we are in communion with God again. It is the gift of the Incarnation, the gift of the gospel, and the gift of Jesus' presence among us always. In Matthew's Gospel the many teachings on forgiveness presume the reality of a community — a group of believers that seek together the kingdom of heaven on earth.

Before we look at this incredible and mysterious gift of forgiveness, let's look at a simple story of a child told by Rachel Naomi Remen, a psychologist who works with the terminally ill and their loved ones, from her collection, *Kitchen Table Wisdom: Stories That Heal*.[1] In her version, a little girl recollects her childhood in New York in first person. I will retell it in third person:

---

1. Rachel Naomi Remen, *Kitchen Table Wisdom: Stories That Heal* (New York: Riverhead Books, 1996, 169–170).

* There once was a little girl who lived in an apartment with a long narrow hallway that led from the front door to the kitchen. A parade of people always came to visit her parents, Jewish doctors active in the movement to create the state of Israel. Guests would stay for hours, talking and drinking coffee, tea, schnapps.

One day her father gave her mother a birthday present that she loved. She put it on a card table in the hallway and every time she would walk by she would bend over it and move things around. All the people who came to visit did the same. They would linger awhile over the table in the hallway on their way to the kitchen. And the girl would wonder what was on the table.

One morning when no one was around, she pulled a chair over and climbed up to see. She had no idea what it was — scattered bits and pieces, a box opened with lots more pieces. A few with straight edges had been stuck together, and all the others had ragged holes. She didn't like it, whatever it was — it had so many dark pieces. She didn't like dark things. She looked around to make sure no one was looking and took a couple. She got down, put them under the cushions of the couch, and removed the chair. Every day, sometimes a couple of times a day, she'd climb up when no one was around, take some pieces and hide them in the couch. After a few days, things started to change. The people who stopped at the table got angry. They punched the wall and stomped their feet and said things she knew you weren't supposed to say — even if you were an adult. She knew that what was on the table was no good.

One day her mother caught her up on her chair looking at the table and its pieces. "Rachel Naomi, what are you doing?" She did not answer. Then her mother laughed and said, "Do you know what this is?"

"Nope."

"It's my birthday present. It's a jigsaw puzzle."

"I don't like it," was all she had to say.

"Why?"

"Because it's dark. Too many dark pieces. It's ugly."

Her mother laughed again. "That's because you don't know what it's supposed to be like when it's all put together and finished." She showed her the cover of the box. It was a picture of the sky in early morning, just before the sun rose. A thin line of light, gold and rose, separated the night sky from the dark sand of a beach. All the rest lay in shadow.

"Oh!" Rachel Naomi said, "That's beautiful — but it doesn't look anything like that!"

Again her mother laughed. "I know. We've been having an awful time putting the thing together. It seems we are missing all kinds of pieces." Rachel Naomi was very quiet. "You wouldn't know anything about that would you?" She was silent still. Her mother laughed again. "Oh, Rachel Naomi, what have you been doing standing on this chair and looking at the puzzle?" The little girl got down, went over to the couch, and pulled the cushions aside. There lay more than a hundred pieces of the puzzle — the darkest ones she could find.

Her mother laughed again and gathered them all up in her apron. They both went back to the puzzle and she dumped them onto the table. And to Rachel Naomi's amazement her mother began to put them all together. She had been looking at the puzzle and working on it for so long that her hands moved quickly and within minutes the gorgeous picture of the sun just about to come up over the beach emerged. Rachel Naomi's eyes grew round and large. "Oh, it's so beautiful!" They both laughed.

Years later, Rachel Naomi reflected on that moment. "That was when I first learned that you can't just take the dark pieces of the puzzle of life and go hide them somewhere under the couch cushions — or anywhere. You have to put the puzzle together that includes them all, otherwise life is full of holes and you never really see the beauty that is always about to burst forth around you."

The Christian community is a group of believers bound in Jesus, in the gospel and its study for conversion of life. They are committed to holding each other accountable for making the gospel become reality in their daily lives through concrete change. They give witness to their faith by their actions, usually the corporal works of mercy. It is not an intentional religious grouping but individuals bound by their belief in Jesus as God's expression of how to live as a human being, and who stake their lives on Jesus' Word as the Truth of God. They endeavor to dwell with one another in the image of the Trinity as the Father, the Son, and the Spirit dwell together as one. The words and practice of Jesus resound, have meaning, and come to fruition among only those who belong to such a group. A parish should contain many of these communities of faith, or base Christian communities. They resemble Russian matryoshka dolls that nest one inside another, or baskets nested one inside another, from tiny ones to larger and larger ones, bearing gifts, food, necessities of life for the world. They are not just groups of people relating to one another, but people serving and sharing with each other, intent on making the world holy.

Christian communities also resemble jigsaw puzzles. The picture on the box reveals what it's supposed to look like when the pieces are fitted together. The gospel, the Word of God, provides a community a vision of how to live in the world. We usually begin a puzzle by linking the straight-edged pieces to give it a shape. These pieces, like those who hold positions of leadership in a community, make sure the puzzle stays together, even though they have fewer holes and hooks than the internal pieces and relate best to others that also have straight edges. The rest of the pieces complete each other, each hole or hook a unique gift that fills up what is lacking in others. Together the pieces of a puzzle exhibit grace and gifts not found in any mere collection of separate individuals.

When assembled, it is obvious whether a puzzle of 500 or 1,000, or even 3,000 pieces is whole, or if any pieces are missing. At any stage of completion, missing pieces call attention to their absence. Just so, in any community most notice the absence of the singular gifts and presence of those not there. Moreover, community is not self-contained. There are other puzzles with their own unique pieces, other communities "close at hand." Taken together, all the puzzles — all the communities of interlocked unique individuals, each community with its own unique vision — are like a quilt that can be sewn together and thrown over a world that needs the warmth and the comfort of God.

The Gospel of Matthew was written for a particular community of believers — one that was struggling to survive in the face of the violent power of the Roman Empire, the hostility of many in the Jewish community, and in the midst of a great deal of fractioning and dissension among themselves. Matthew's Gospel is written to give this group so at odds with themselves and others an identity that would allow them to become graceful and enduring in the world, living out the Word of Jesus and becoming the kingdom of heaven in the world — held together by the presence of the Risen Lord with them all days.

One segment of Matthew's Gospel (it appears in only Matthew's account) must be seen in light of the true nature of community and how this community struggled to survive fifty or more years after the death and resurrection of Jesus. Against this segment are set all subsequent gospel teachings on community and on the forgiveness that lies at the heart of community. It is called Peter's "profession of faith" where in the name of the church — Matthew's community — he is entrusted with responsibility for the keys of the kingdom. In the previous chapter, when Jesus had walked across storm-tossed water to his community, Peter gets out of the boat and attempts to walk on the water as well. He "feels" the force of the wind, takes fright and — taking his eyes off Jesus — begins to sink. He cries out, "Lord! Save me!" Immediately, Jesus stretched out his hand and caught him. Jesus said, "O you of little faith, why did you doubt?" After they got into the boat, the wind died down (Mt 14:30–33). This is the one entrusted with the keys of the kingdom!

This segment begins (as does Mark's account) in Caesarea Philippi, where Jesus puts the question to his disciples that forces them to say who they think he is. Prophet? Teacher?

> "Who do people say that the Son of Man is?" They replied, "Some say John the Baptist, others, Elijah, still others Jeremiah or one of the prophets." He said to them, "But who do

you say that I am?" Simon Peter said in reply, "You are the
Messiah, the Son of the living God." Jesus said to him in
reply: "Blessed are you, Simon son of Jonah. For flesh
and blood has not revealed this to you, but my heavenly
Father." (Mt 16:13–17)

Jesus' question and the disciples' answers provide an important
context for what follows. Most people, including the disciples themselves who use other people's words in their answer, believe that
Jesus is a prophet, yet another in the long tradition of prophets. The
prophets teach the true nature of worship of God, the care of the
poor, and the coming of the kingdom of justice and peace into the
world. Like God, a prophet sees these three as one and the same.
True worship is to care for the poor, and caring for the poor brings
the kingdom of peace and justice, the only worship that God wants
from his people. But Jesus wants his followers to dig deeper. He
wants them to articulate who *they* think he is — they who have been
close to him, listening to his words, praying with him, intimate to his
daily life. Simon Peter (the name designates both who he is before
meeting Jesus and who he is as a disciple) is the one who answers.
This is the Peter of little faith, easily frightened amidst storm and
wind, the one who cries out, "Save me!" His answer affirms what
Matthew's community believed about Jesus: "You are the Messiah,
the Son of the living God." The Messiah, the title given to Jesus —
the fulfillment of all the prophecies about the one who is to come —
the presence of God so clearly with his people in justice and peace
that all the nations see Israel as a light in the world and come to learn
from Jerusalem the wisdom of God. He is the Son of the living God
— the words of the Voice at Jesus' baptism, the Beloved. He adds
the word "living" because from the beginning the God of Israel is
always referred to as the God of the Living — of all the living — the
God of Abraham, Isaac, and Jacob, David and the kings, the
prophets and all the people. Peter is proclaiming Jesus as he is
described at the end of the genealogy, Jesus who is called the Christ.
When he says, "You are ... the Son of ... God" Peter is the first to

declare Jesus' identity as stated in words from Hebrew Scripture and from the Voice at his baptism. Many overlook the way Jesus phrases his question. He asks, "Who do people say that the Son of Man is?" This is who Jesus believes himself to be, how he will refer to himself over and over again as he mentions his passion and death on the cross and as he renders judgment in the parables. And this is the Jesus, the Son of Man that Peter will vehemently deny three times.[2]

Jesus Responds to Peter's Answer:

"Blessed are you, Simon son of Jonah. For flesh and blood has not revealed this to you, but my heavenly Father. And so I say to you, you are Peter, and upon this rock I will build my church, and the gates of the netherworld shall not prevail against it. I will give you the keys to the kingdom of heaven. Whatever you bind on earth shall be bound in heaven; and whatever you loose on earth shall be loosed in heaven." Then he strictly ordered his disciples to tell no one that he was the Messiah. (Mt 16:17b–20)

For over two thousand years these words have been interpreted in diverse ways, some of which take us away from Matthew's original reasons for recording them. He wrote them to build an identity for his community. Who are they after the destruction of the Temple, the dissolution of Jewish tradition and ritual associated with the synagogue, having been severed from their families and from the Jewish nation and its religious structures by their choice to follow Christ? Who are they as they seek to become believers in Jesus in the face of domination by the Romans? And who are they as they dispute among themselves about their Jewish identity — what must be kept and what must be left behind as they fill themselves with the new wine, as they clothe themselves with the new cloth of Jesus' experience and his teaching and interpretation of the Law and the Prophets? Matthew

---

2. See my further discussion of Son of Man in chapter 9.

cites these words of Jesus to reinforce his community in the face of powerful currents that threatened the fledgling Christian community. The word that Matthew uses to describe his community-as-church — *ekklesia* — is a Greek term that means "a gathering" or "a meeting." It names what the followers of Jesus became after Jesus' death and resurrection as they came together as a community persecuted by the Roman Empire, excluded and shunned by the Jewish leadership, and as they struggled among themselves to interpret Jesus' words and live them in the world. Matthew is telling his community that Jesus is with them and that nothing can stand against them: not the Roman Empire, not the Jewish leadership, not their own infighting and lack of faith, not even the gates of hell — they will survive, with grace (the power and authority of the Holy Spirit) and with all that they need to preach and to be the gospel for all the world.

Peter is given in trust the keys to the kingdom of heaven — the teachings and the hope that unlock all that Jesus has been sharing with his disciples, preaching to them and announcing as "close at hand" in his own presence, in his own word and in his own flesh, his body. And the core of that gospel, that relationship with God and one another, the essence of the kingdom of heaven, is forgiveness. The gift of forgiveness works in two ways: binding and loosing. It holds bound, accountable, those in the community, the kingdom of heaven; and it also looses them, sets them free.

Matthew's next chapter contains the discourse on community — how it lives, survives together, grows, matures, and becomes holy. That discourse is all about forgiveness — the glue, the authority, the Spirit that binds the community together as well as the power, the Spirit that unties and frees them. One man, Peter, is entrusted with the keys in the name of the community perhaps because he more than many others needs those keys and the gift of forgiveness that they signify. His faith is weak, he has betrayed Jesus three times, he is thick and slow to understand and accept the forgiveness and mercy that Jesus teaches and demands of his community.

The Greatest in the Kingdom

The chapter on forgiveness begins with Jesus placing a child in front of his disciples and telling them forthrightly, solemnly, that "unless you turn and become like children you will not enter the kingdom of heaven. Whoever humbles himself like this child is the greatest in the kingdom of heaven" (Mt 18:1–4). This is the doorway into the kingdom, the entrance to community, the pre-requisite for church. Recall the position at that time of children in Jewish society — the least in the community, dependent, obedient, at others' beck and call, vulnerable to abuse and violence, ignored, left without necessities, endangered by outsiders as well as by those within the community who failed to care for them. A child, the child of our Father, the brother or sister of Jesus, is the least in the world, the expendable one, the one who falls through the cracks, the unknown or neglected one, the one who needs most the Good News in Jesus that all are beloved children of God. At the final judgment we will be measured against children such as these to determine whether we end up among the sheep or the goats. Jesus is clear — each of his listeners, and all of them together must strive "to become like children" in order to enter. In the Sermon on the Mount he told them to enter by the narrow gate and that the hard road leads to life. And he told them that only a few find it (Mt 7:13–14).

Just before Jesus admonishes his disciples to dwell and grow in community life as God's children, as his brothers and sisters, he gives them a simple yet demanding lesson that lays the theological foundation of all that follows: the parable of the lost sheep:

> What is your opinion? If a man has a hundred sheep and one of them goes astray, will he not leave the ninety-nine in the hills and go in search of the stray? And if he finds it, amen, I say to you, he rejoices more over it than over the ninety-nine that did not stray. In just the same way, it is not the will of your heavenly Father that one of these little ones be lost. (Mt 18:12–14)

This parable and many of Jesus' other teachings suggest at least two ways to become a little child. One way is to take our place among the least of our brothers and sisters: the poor, the condemned, the shunned, the victims of violence, the children of the Beatitudes — those who never know justice and who struggle for mere survival in a scornful world that considers them expendable or unnecessary. The other way, through our relation to our Father begun in baptism, is to become more and more a child of God, like Jesus, the Son of Man, the Crucified one, who relies only on the power and the authority of God. All of us are sinners, and even after we know that we are the beloved children of God we continue to sin often, sometimes gravely, always affecting the others — the ninety-nine.

Consider the question Jesus poses in this parable. One of your sheep strays but you have ninety-nine more. Would you leave them alone and go off after the one, knowing that doing so leaves the others vulnerable to weather, wild animals, thieves and poachers, even their own tendencies to bolt in panic at the slightest thing that startles them? Is the one that strays so crucial, so necessary to the rest of the group that it's worth the effort and the risk to leave the others in order to pursue it? Anyone who has worked with sheep knows that if a lone sheep gets lost or in trouble it usually just lies down and waits for the shepherd to come and get it. It brays and whines, but does nothing to find its way back to the fold or to get out of whatever rut, bog, or trouble it has gotten itself into. Likewise, it takes very little to stampede a herd of sheep, and when they do they trample their young as they scatter wildly in every direction.

The parable poses a dilemma. Is the stray — the sinner, the problem, the miscreant, the disordered troublemaker — more important than the group at large? Or even more to the point, doesn't the return of the one that strays, the lost one, the sinner, reconfirm the integrity of the group? The shepherd rejoices in the lost sheep found, more than in any who don't stray! And it is the will of our Father that not even one single person gets lost. Consider the implications of this parable for our churches, parishes, or communities today. At one time or another, sometimes often, each of us is the straying sheep. Yet because most of us think that we don't stray and don't think much of those that do, we fail to recognize, understand, or accept that the Shepherd rejoices more in the lost than he does in those of us who have not strayed! And how do we act when the stray returns or is brought back (not to mention those who stray again and again)? This is the background for Jesus' preaching and advice on how the community is to live together in the power and authority of our Father and the Spirit of God with him.

Matthew next presents a program for dealing with those who dissent, with anyone harmed or sinned against, anyone who feels wronged. It intensifies to the point of an unbearable confrontation — and instructs what to do if no resolution can be reached. This is the process:

First, have it out with the other alone, one on one. If the other listens, you've won your brother or sister back into the kingdom of heaven, into the sheepfold, into the community.

Then, if the other does not listen, return with one or two others: the testimony of two or three witnesses is required to sustain any charge. You may not just take a friend who will side with you on the issue or even two to gang up on the other person. Making the issue public requires impartial witnesses and evidence.

If that does not work, report the dispute to the community. This presupposes that you and the other both already have a relationship with a community that holds its members accountable for their words and actions. Some translations of Matthew's Gospel suggest as the next step that leaders within the community, not the community itself, should deal with such matters; if the leaders could not resolve it, then it was to be taken to the community at large.

As a last resort, if the person accused of wrongdoing does not listen and repent, all are to "treat the person as a pagan or a tax collector" (Mt 18:15–17).

But note how Jesus treats pagans and tax collectors — with the greatest care and tender regard. The primary focus of grace and work is to leave the ninety-nine, the rest of the community, and to reach out to those considered straying or lost. Jesus is concerned about them, eats with them first, honors them more, and invites his disciples to join him with them. They must realize that without them there really isn't any community, only a group of people who all agree to agree on the same things, and exclude and blame the others.

A short Hasidic story illustrates how to handle disputes, especially in family and community.

> *   A young father, learning how to interpret and practice the Torah in relation to his own wayward child, comes to his rabbi with a question: "Rabbi, what am I to do? He's disobedient and surly. He's rebellious and he violates some of the laws in the Torah, the Talmud, and in the tradition. He even does just stupid things. He disagrees with what I say and he does what he knows will annoy me or hurt me. He spends time with people I abhor and think are evil-doers. What can I do?"
>
> The rabbi looked at him with great compassion and said: "Love him more!"

Jesus is saying the same to us. We reveal whether we are the beloved children of God, the brothers and sisters of Jesus, by how we treat the members of our own family, parish, community, and church, not to mention outsiders, the poor, or even enemies. If we do not set aside our own issues and habits and structures to make sure that these others are searched for, sought out, taken care of, welcomed back, and loved more, then we are not the children of our Father; we are just a lot of sheep that happen to flock together.

The words he spoke to Peter Jesus repeats to the disciples, to the entire community: "Amen I say to you, whatever you bind on earth shall be bound in heaven, and whatever you loose on earth shall be loosed in heaven" (Mt 18:18). It is up to us to bind and hold together the community, the children of our Father. We will be held responsible and accountable for all we have kept with us and for all we have lost and not gone after with the care, love, and joy of the Shepherd, our brother Jesus. And what follows is connected to this exhortation and has to be interpreted in light of all that has gone before. Jesus tells them — and us: "Amen, I say to you, if two of you agree on earth about anything for which they are to pray, it shall be granted to them by my heavenly Father. For where two or three are gathered together in my name, there am I in the midst of them" (Mt 18:19–20).

What are we praying for? What are we agreeing to ask for? When we gather in twos and threes and small communities, what are we working on? Jesus' presence is among us, as the children of our Father. We must ask for the art and grace of being anguished by those who stray, so that we can go after them and love them more. We must ask for skill and faithfulness in forgiveness and keeping the community together, even when people have been wronged or when we think others have strayed. We cannot shun anyone and we cannot blame them, accuse them, humiliate them, or leave them outside the protection and the sanctuary of the community. We are responsible for each other, most especially for sinners, the straying, the lost. This must be our prayer — to learn understanding and how to listen to others again and again, and never to exclude, separate ourselves from others or put others out or segregate them from the life of the community, denying them word and manna because we disagree with them or because we think they have done wrong.

This interpretation makes some people react with anger and self-righteousness. In the text Peter does exactly that — he has difficulty accepting Jesus' words. He hears what Jesus is saying but does not really listen. Peter wants specific boundaries on what he has to do in community with anyone, in regards to any wrongdoing. Peter reacts and thinks like we do:

> Then Peter approaching asked him, "Lord, if my brother sins against me, how often must I forgive him? As many as seven times?" Jesus answered, "I say to you not seven times but seventy-seven times." (Mt 18:22)

Peter wants the least he has to do in order to comply with Jesus' words. He is missing the point. He thinks he's generous in offering seven as the number of times to forgive. Seven of course is a complete number — seven days for creation! But Jesus insists: stop counting and start forgiving. This is a lifestyle, a way of relating, of looking at one another, at all our brothers and sisters, especially those with whom we are angry and who we don't want to see, talk with, listen to, or continue relating to. Whether translated "seven times seven times" or "seventy-seven times," Jesus is not naming any number that we can stop at — it is limitless. We are to forgive one another as our Father forgives us. Simply. Directly. Without doubt or equivocation. We are not to play games with numbers. The Good News is we are forgiven in Jesus for everything, all of us; in the Our Father we pray that our God forgive us as we forgive one another.

It is important to note that the petition in the Our Father, "forgive us our debts, as we forgive those who are in debt to us," uses two different words for "debt." The first connotes a huge amount — something that could never be repaid, impossible to forgive, drop, or cancel. This is the debt each of us owes God, and we are not to forget that God's massive generosity in forgiving it utterly for all of us is the kingdom of heaven, in the person and presence of Jesus among us. The second word in the petition for debt connotes a piddling amount, a trifle, a couple of dollars perhaps — which is what any other human being owes any of us. We live as forgiven and loved children. If we believe in Jesus, the beloved Son of God, we are to live with each other as forgiven and loved brothers and sisters.

Jesus' gospel, Jesus' life, Jesus' presence tell us repeatedly that we must learn to look at all the dark pieces of our lives and of the lives of others, all that happens in the world, and all people with the eyes of God, with the eyes of forgiveness, with the eyes of our Father who sees us all as his beloved children. Our God, our Father and our brother, Jesus, in the Spirit of God never consider anyone lost. The following chapter will take up the next two phases in this gift of forgiveness: reconciliation and atonement — in its original meaning, "at-one-ment," communion, the unity of the community of the kingdom of heaven. This chapter on God's treasured gift to us — forgiveness — ends with a story within a story within a story. It is from the tradition of the Baal Shem Tov, whose name means The Master of the Good Name, who, much as Jesus did, told stories to his disciples to teach them how to act and what they must remember. This story is called "Someone Waits for Your Story to Be Told."

* A young man wanted to become a disciple of Baal Shem Tov and stay in his community. He was awed by the Master's learning and knowledge, but even more so by his compassion and mercy to all who came to him. For he had many students and even more visitors, the curious, the anxious in need of counsel, those who came to dispute him or contradict him or make fun of him and discredit him, but always he was kind, listened respectfully, and responded with grace. As he stayed with the Baal Shem Tov the young man came to realize that his place was not in this community. He had learned that he was to be an itinerant preacher who brought the message of the Baal Shem Tov to faraway places. He would travel as a simple merchant, selling books and items that everyone always needed or always needed to have repaired, like scissors, hammers, awls, pincers, and tongs.

When the young man knew it was time to take leave of his teacher, while waiting in line to say goodbye and receive his blessing, a distressed man barged right in, shoving his way to the front of the line. The Baal Shem Tov signaled that he was to be allowed to come in before everyone else and spent a long time with him. The man left still anxious and unaware of everyone around him, but the Baal Shem Tov had obviously eased some of his distress. When the young man finally reached the front of the line, his master blessed and embraced him. And just before he left, the Baal Shem Tov told him, "Remember what you have seen here, not just all the time you have been here, but especially today, with this man who came in such need. For you will never know when someone desperately needs what you have to tell him." And so the young man went his way for years and decades, doing his work, repairing tools, and telling his stories long after the Baal Shem Tov himself had died.

One winter night he was cold and hungry. No one seemed to need his services or tools. No one even wanted his stories. In a tavern he tried to tell some of his tales in exchange for food, drink, and lodging, but they'd heard them all before. Someone did tell him, "Go down the road a ways and you'll see a huge house, lighted within — you can't miss it. The man who lives there pays for stories! A kopeck for every story and you've got lots ... you'll eat and drink well tonight and you'll have the best bed in town." And so the man made his way back into the cold night. He easily found the house they spoke of and when he knocked, someone answered immediately. He stated his purpose — he had stories to tell. He was ushered into a great dining room, with a long narrow table set with abundant food and drink. A place was set at one end and at the other a man sat in the shadows. The storyteller sat down and food was handed to him. The man spoke: "Tell me stories." For every story, the host shoved a kopeck down the table. As the man ate and drank to his heart's content, his pile of coins grew and grew. But his host's discomfort grew too. Each story made him more agitated, impatient to get onto the next. Finally the storyteller ran out of stories. He'd been there for hours. He couldn't think of any more.

The man at the other end of the table rose and told him it was time to leave. With the money he had made that night, he could find lodging in one of the inns. The storyteller got up, but just as he was going out the door he turned and said, "I do have one more story, one I've never told before." The man came closer. He told of the Baal Shem Tov and the agitated man so unaware as he barged in, yet how the Baal Shem Tov listened and took him in before all the others who had been waiting in line for hours. He always remembered the look on the man's face as he left — eased and softened though he was still upset. And as he finished this last tale, the storyteller realized that tears were flowing freely down the man's cheeks. The man cried, "I am that man!" It was time for the storyteller to listen in amazement. The man told him how he had betrayed his faith and stopped practicing and praying as a Jew so he could make money and rise in society. He became a Christian, but wanted to be a Jew again. But now many people relied on him. If he went back to being a Jew they would all suffer and might even be in danger because of his actions. He went to the Baal Shem Tov to find out what he could do. The Baal Shem Tov embraced him and told him to begin practicing and living as a

Jew, but in secret so that others around him would not be aware. He was to do penance, to give alms graciously, to remember always his betrayal of his faith. And one day, someone would come to him and tell him his own story — his encounter with the Baal Shem Tov. When he heard that story, he would know that he had been forgiven, but also that his sin and his debt was paid. He would be free again, as a Jew belonging to God. The two fell into each others' arms and for days spoke of their Master and how to live in the world in spite of the hostility and persecution of their people.

You never know when another waits for you to tell a story. Others, so many others depend on whether or not we believe, remember, and tell of the goodness and forgiveness of our God. It is so with us, the beloved children of our Father. Someone waits. Someone is always waiting for us to share the good news of forgiveness and to tell the gospel of forgiveness. Someone waits. Are we telling the story with our lives and acceptance, only as a last resort using words?

Questions

1. Do you find it harder to forgive someone else, or to ask for forgiveness for what you have done? Why?

2. Have you ever felt the need to ask forgiveness from a group — or as a group, community, or parish to ask forgiveness for what you have done or neglected to do?

3. When you gather as two or three, in Jesus' name, do you pray for the grace and the strength to forgive others? Who in your community, parish, family, workplace, school, and country do you need to forgive now?

4. Do you believe that those who stray are the most important in the community? What does it mean for you and for your church community to love these people more in practical ways? Or, like Peter, do you feel a bit put out by Jesus' command?

6
Reconciliation and At-One-Ment: The Other Gifts of Forgiveness

Forgiveness is only the first of three levels of this gift from the Father, in Jesus' Spirit. The journey to forgiveness itself can be long and arduous, or on rare occasions its levels can be experienced quickly, even simultaneously. Whether they transpire over time or happen all at once, a person seeking to forgive another must go through four steps.

1. *To forgo* — to forgo vengeance, name-calling, complaining, telling others about what has happened, bitter words and feelings, anger, retaliation—anything that would aggravate the situation further.

2. *To forbear* — to accept our share of the burden of forgiveness, bearing wrongs patiently, with equanimity, with good will and simple human courtesy, refusing to stack the deck against the other or connect the present situation to any past grievances.

3. *To forget* — to create new memories so that the next time we encounter the person his or her transgression or injustice toward you is not the first thing we remember or react to. We can do this by reaching out in concrete ways: a cup of coffee,

a card, a movie or another shared experience — something inserted into the frame of reference that allows us to relate to the other and to create a new opening for the future.

4. *To forgive* — to give, to pass on to others as God has done for us the grace we have been given, each act of forgiveness drawing us deeper into the gift of forgiveness that our God gives us in Jesus.

Throughout the entire process we must pray for the person we intend to and need to forgive. If we do not forgive we remain imprisoned in our own emotions, in the past and what we perceive as done to us, instead of living in the freedom of the children of God, able to pass on to others what has been given to us by God, not merely throwing back at them what we feel they have done to us. When we face injustice, sin, and evil we are never ever to "do unto others what they have done unto us." We are to do unto others what God has done and is doing unto us. We are to live as people of the gift of forgiveness.

This is the first level of the gift. Each concrete act of forgiveness is aimed toward a second level that results in mutuality, called "reconciliation," which in Greek means, "to walk together again." In the most powerful of the gospels' reconciliation stories, toward the end of the Gospel of John, the resurrected Jesus walks the beach with Peter. Jesus addresses him as "Simon, son of John," his name and identity before they ever met. Peter, who betrayed Jesus three times, with ever more intensity and vehemence must assert his love three times to walk with Jesus again as his follower and friend. Forgiveness is a given. The real work begins with reconciliation, walking together again. Everything is forgivable and redeemable, but it is hard work to keep the community whole.

During times of persecution and martyrdom, many in the early church lived in fear that if arrested they might bow to the power of Rome and give up their faith, committing the sin of apostasy. Some who did betray the faith, however, often having turned other members of the community into the authorities as well, later wanted to come back.

Some leaders refused to forgive apostates, but others did so in the name of the community. Christians condemned to torture and death in the public arena were imprisoned until it was time for their martyrdom. Those who sought to repent their apostasy could witness to their faith by asking those facing death to forgive them and to pray for them as they died. They knew that the faith of the martyrs, who they watched die gruesome deaths, reconciled them to the community. After the martyr was buried, the community welcomed the apostate back, forgiven because of the martyr's mercy. No sin is unforgivable. Members of the community (all of whom have been entrusted with the keys of forgiveness) can forgive and draw back into the sanctuary those who have sinned.

Just after telling Peter that to be a Christian he must forgive not seven times, but seventy-seven times — that is, without limit — Jesus pronounces a startling, seemingly harsh parable. It speaks of the "kingdom of heaven," which means it deals with how we live now on earth in the kingdom and how we witness to the world the way in which the kingdom comes and abides among us. Some call it "the parable of the unforgiving debtor":

> That is why the kingdom of heaven may be likened to a king who decided to settle accounts with his servants. When he began the accounting, a debtor was brought before him who owed him a huge amount. Since he had no way of paying it back, his master ordered him to be sold, along with his wife, his children and all his property, in payment of the debt. At that, the servant fell down, did him homage, and said, "Be patient with me, and I will pay you back in full." Moved with compassion the master of that servant let him go and forgave him the loan. (Mt 18:23–28)

Because it is a parable, it starts off stating the obvious: a situation, circumstance, or problem familiar to those who hear the story. Then, out of nowhere, comes something totally unexpected, even preposterous — something that wouldn't or didn't happen in reality. The situation was familiar — a man in debt way over his means and unable to repay faced the usual consequence — being sold into slavery to satisfy the debt. Such an event was common. But then the first surprise comes: the master has such pity on the servant that he drops the entire debt — which is massive. Some translations mention a specific amount, ten thousand talents. A talent was the largest denomination of gold currency, and he owes ten thousand! There would have been gasps all around. What kind of king is this? Jesus would have had their undivided attention:

> When that servant had left, he found one of his fellow servants who owed him a much smaller amount. He seized him and started to choke him, demanding, "Pay back what you owe." Falling to his knees, his fellow servant begged him, "Be patient with me, and I will pay you back." But he refused. Instead, he had him put in prison until he paid back the debt. Now when his fellow servants saw what had happened, they were deeply disturbed, and went to their master and reported the whole affair. (Mt 18:28–32)

The two scenarios are almost identical, except the levels of power and authority and the amount of debt have dropped drastically. The servant on the same level as the servant just freed from his enormous burden also begs mercy. But it seems the freed servant has a short memory and no gratitude for what his master, the king, has done for him. He will not follow the king's lead on how to live with others. Instead he imposes what a king usually would have done to him, destroying a fellow servant's life (as well as his family's). This, in many ways, resembles what happens in the world. What goes around doesn't necessarily come around — we learn slowly, especially in regard to gratitude. Again, however, the parable presents something surprising and startling: now the other servants are the ones deeply distressed. Having seen and come to know their king in his graciousness to the indebted servant, they want him to know what has happened — their ungrateful fellow servant did not pass along the king's gift. He took for granted what he had received and insulted the king's magnanimity. The freed servant may not have changed his behavior because of what has been granted him, but the other servants will not let his injustice to another go unnoticed:

His master summoned him and said to him, "You wicked
servant! I forgave you your entire debt because you begged
me to. Should you not have had pity on your fellow servant,
as I had pity on you?" Then in anger his master handed him
over to the torturers until he should pay back the whole
debt. So will my heavenly Father do to you, unless each of
you forgives his brother from his heart. (Mt 18:33–35)

This is the third and the most unnerving aspect of the parable —
something none of us want to hear or accept as the Word of Jesus. The
servant is summoned and made to answer for his own actions and his
wrongdoing after the king's generosity to him. God treats us with
mercy and pity; we are to learn to imitate our God and treat one another
likewise. If we accept the gift of forgiveness then we must proffer that
same gift to all others, or else — or else justice requires that we be
treated just as we treat others. As horrifying and dismaying as it may
be, this is the truth. We are always forgiven and we are often quick to
take the gift, but how often do we not give that gift to others? We
persist in our stingy, self-righteous, demanding, and violent dealings
with others, even after we have known such incredible graciousness
from our God. This judgment upon the servant who does not heed and
reciprocate what he himself has experienced from the king echoes
Jesus' words in the Sermon on the Mount:

Stop judging, that you may not be judged. For as you judge,
so will you be judged, and the measure with which you
measure will be measured out to you. Why do you notice the
splinter in your brother's eye, but do not perceive the wooden
beam in your own eyes? How can you say to your brother,
"Let me remove that splinter from your eye," while the
wooden beam is in your eye? You hypocrite, remove the
wooden beam from your eye first; then you will see clearly to
remove the splinter from your brother's eye. (Mt 7:1–5)

In all our dealings with others we must reflect how God knows each
of us and never fails to shower us with forgiveness. We must share
forgiveness among ourselves as lavishly as God has given it to us. If

not, we will receive the same justice we have done unto others. If we refuse to forgive others, we will be held accountable. This is what this sobering parable, the Word of God, exhorts. Jesus warns that we must forgive our brothers and sisters from our hearts.

In the early church every sin, no matter how grave, could be forgiven and the forgiven sinner drawn back into the community — reconciled. The very early church thought that one didn't sin after baptism! That error was soon realized and so all the baptized came to practice the three disciplines that Jesus preached in his first sermon: prayer, fasting, and almsgiving. Through them, along with celebration and reception of the Eucharist, sins of the baptized were forgiven. Breaking the word and breaking the bread in community brought about the forgiveness of the sins of the community.

Reconciliation is founded upon the practice of almsgiving and its function both in forgiving sin and in determining how we ourselves view sinners who need to be forgiven. Our communities have always shunned certain factions or individuals because they are considered sinners. A Jewish story can serve to caution us when we are tempted to make judgments about sin and sinners, and when we wonder whether everyone in our community deserves our forgiveness. It is called "Yossele the Miser."

> * Once a very rich man, Yossele, was considered a stingy, mean miser. Everyone was sure that he shared his wealth with no one, never gave to anyone — ever. Everyone in the ghetto where he lived knew how much he had and how he hoarded it, and everyone judged him for not doing something to help the suffering and need of the women and the children and the elderly. But he never made public donations. They thought he was hard-hearted, and they hated him for it. They talked about him and his stinginess and prayed that God, blest be His Name, would remember his meanness. The children feared him and threw stones at him when he walked in the street. Yossele, like everyone else, eventually got old and sick. The word spread that he was finally nearing the end. Before he died the community burial society went to him and asked for the ritual gift of a thou-

sand rubles for the poor. He turned his head to the wall, refusing even to speak with them. So they left him and he died alone.

After his death they searched his big house, but could find no money at all, and so they buried him outside the community in an unmarked paupers' grave, a fitting end, they thought, for a man who had not recognized the poor while he lived.

But then disturbing changes began to surface. Just before the Sabbath, the community leaders started approaching the rabbi for money to be given to poor women and children and old people. He gave them what he could, when he could. But he asked them, "What did you do before? Why are you asking me now? You never did previously." The rabbi began making inquires. To his horror he found that every week before the Sabbath Yossele had been secretly giving to the poor so that they did not have to beg from the leaders or the rabbi. And he had given so that no one, not even those who received his generosity, would know.

The rabbi was distressed. Yossele had been the holiest of them of all and now they didn't even know where he was buried. They had treated him so vilely — doing to him what they had accused him of, blaming him for what really was their own shallow judgment and smallness of mind and heart. The rabbi gathered the whole community and decreed that they must fast and do penance for what they had done to Yossele while he was alive and for how they had dishonored him in death. They must ask Yossele to forgive them their mean-spiritedness — and they must ask for some sign that they were forgiven. They all set to it with fervor.

After fasting for some time, the rabbi fell into a trance. And behold in a vision he saw Yossele in the Garden of Eden surrounded by the righteous. Yossele told him, "Tell the people to stop fasting and doing penance and to go home and live with each other. I have forgiven them. I forgave them every day for what they did and what they thought of me. You see, long ago I asked God, blest be His Name, for a favor. I wanted the honor and the privilege of giving to others the way God gives, without anyone's knowledge and without requiring anyone's thanks. I wanted them to be so thankful that they in turn would give out of their bounty to others also in need." The rabbi was stunned. When he told the people what he had seen and heard they were speechless. What did they know? There was so much to learn. So much to change!

The story warns us all to be careful in judging others and to practice reconciliation. As individuals and as church we must first look to ourselves and take care about how we approach others, judge others, and treat others.

The early church considered "sin" to mean "missing the mark," this mark being to aim at the practice of true worship, faithfulness and obedience to the Word of Jesus. Over its first three hundred years a "Rite of Penitents" developed by which members whose sin was so grievous that it had affected the whole community could be reconciled. Only certain sins were considered so destructive that a sinner must enroll in this Rite to be brought back into communion. These sins, which affected the community's own sense of itself and made it harder for the rest of the church to believe and practice, included offenses such as apostasy, violence toward others, adultery, fornication, refusal to forgive, greediness and hoarding, and failure to put the gifts of the Spirit at the service of the community.

The Rite of Penitents itself followed a simple process of forgiveness and reconciliation: acknowledgement of guilt, spoken request for forgiveness, conversion of one's life and restitution, penance in the form of a positive action to correct the previous sinful behavior or attitude, and thanksgiving for the goodness and mercy of God who is Forgiveness and Mercy in Jesus.

Subsequent chapters of Matthew's Gospel deal with specific categories of sin: unfaithfulness in marriage and all relationships; the misuse of money and the danger of riches; and the negative effects on the community of personal sin such as scandal, discouragement, and despair. Leaders' sins caused further problems, because their hypocrisy devastated the spirit of the community. The church suffered from external tensions and pressures imposed on it by the Roman Empire and the Jewish leaders. Far worse, however, was the tension and despair within the community caused by believers who mistreated one another despite their baptism and their sharing the Word and the Bread of life. The prophetic ideal of the gospel was livable — Jesus' words could be obeyed and lived.

The power of the Spirit never left the community. Certain "marks" or behaviors characterized the life of a believer. Echoing the Ten Commandments, there were ten such marks:

1. *Forgive* everyone, everything, always, seventy times seven times. "Stop counting and start forgiving" is a way of life for the children of God.

2. *Love one another as I have loved you* — Love even unto death. What you believe may cost your life. Believing in and practicing love has no limit.

3. *Love your enemies — do no harm to anyone* — Respond to evil, sin and injustice without violence. Do good to others, bless those who curse you, return goodness for evil.

4. *There are to be no poor among you* — Give to all who beg from you. Share your excess and practice the virtue of poverty. "Whatever you did for one of these least brothers of mine, you did for me" (Mt 25:40).

5. *Deny yourself* so that you do not deny Jesus. Offer your sufferings for the healing of nations and for others. Pick up your cross and follow Jesus.

6. *Bear one another's burdens* and seek to relieve all human misery. Practice the corporal works of mercy.

7. *Be truthful* and live with integrity of word, practice, thought, and public witness.

8. *Be the Good News of God for the poor*. Heal, feed, welcome all to community, provide sanctuary, and accept everyone as the Body of Christ.

9. *Atone for evil,* your own, others', the church's, and the world's. This means at-one-ment, keeping the community at one as well as doing restoration and working for justice in the world.

10. *In everything, in every situation, in every relationship, remember:* "I came so that they might have life and have it more abundantly" (Jn 10:10). This is the defining concept in all decisions and practice, and it is worded in the plural — Jesus came not just for individuals, but for groups, for all peoples.

These marks of the Christian describe the pattern of life that all are called to in baptism. And all fail, often and miserably, at living up to baptismal vows. Relating to sinners (that is, all of us) is always the tension between teaching and preaching the prophetic truth of who we are as the beloved children of God and the pastoral response to the fact that we fail continually. We are forgiven sinners.

The third level of forgiveness is at-one-ment, the communion of the believers that is preserved, deepened, and extended through forgiveness and reconciliation. Jesus speaks of forgiveness and community, and his call to his followers to be faithful in marriage and in all their relationships, to be gracious in sharing what they have been given with the poor and respond to the invitation to "be perfect" like our heavenly Father — holy, compassionate, merciful and forgiving and loving (see Mt 19). The parable that follows is a parable on community — on being in communion with each other and atoning with and for each other so that the community can be truly at-one in Jesus, to the glory of the Father in the power of the Spirit. The parable deals with the owner of a vineyard and his workers. Only Matthew includes it in his gospel, so it is focused toward his own community, made up of people from different backgrounds and traditions:

> The kingdom of heaven is like a landowner who went out at dawn to hire laborers for his vineyard. After agreeing with them for the usual daily wage, he sent them into his vineyard. Going out about nine o'clock, he saw others standing idle in the marketplace, and he said to them, "You too go into my vineyard and I will pay you what is just." So they went off. (And) he went out again around noon, and around three o'clock and did likewise. Going out about five o'clock, he found others standing around, and said to them,

"Why do you stand here idle all day?" They answered, "Because no one has hired us." He said to them, "You too go into my vineyard." (Mt 20:1–8)

This was the routine for many day laborers at the time. At harvest time many more workers were needed to bring in the grapes before the weather changed or they rotted on the vines. Extra workers who had no permanent jobs would assemble in the middle of the village and wait to be hired. The usual day's wage was one denarius. The first batch of laborers would be sent out as early as possible before the heat became unbearable. But more and more laborers would be needed as the day wore on and those hired earlier began to weaken, or the grapes were not coming in as fast as needed. The earlier you went to work, the more you were paid. The first group knows — it's a full denarius. The second group will get whatever the owner decides is fair, as will the next two. And with the last group the vineyard owner makes no mention of what they will get. But the owner has complete control over the vineyard, the workers, the crop, and much that transpires in the village itself.

Jesus' listeners would know the scene well. Moreover, the vineyard had long been used as a metaphor for the relationship between Israel and Yahweh God who is always looking for the fruit of the covenant with the people of God. The crop is all-important — without grapes, there will be no wine, nothing to drink and celebrate with. The vineyard exists to bear fruit. As the familiar story continues his audience would begin to be shocked, as we still are today:

When it was evening the owner of the vineyard said to his foreman, "Summon the laborers and give them their pay, beginning with the last and ending with the first." When those who had started about five o'clock came, each received the usual daily wage. So when the first came, they thought that they would receive more, but each of them also got the usual wage. And on receiving it they grumbled against the landowner, saying, "These last ones worked only one hour, and you have made them equal to us, who bore the day's burden and the heat." (Mt 20:9–12)

The first shock is that those who come last are paid first instead of those who worked the longest (and supposedly the hardest). The second is that those who worked one hour, or three or four or nine all get paid the same! Each group that came forward expected more because they had worked more. The group that worked all day (probably from four in the morning to four in the afternoon) definitely expect to get paid more, but the foreman gives them only what they contracted for, what everyone else has gotten. Thoroughly put out and annoyed, they complain loudly and angrily directly to the vineyard owner, not to the one handing out the pay:

> He said to one of them in reply, "My friend, I am not cheating you. Did you not agree with me for the usual daily wage? Take what is yours and go. What if I wish to give this last one the same as you? (Or) am I not free to do as I wish with my own money? Are you envious because I am generous?" Thus the last will be first, and the first will be last. (Mt 20:13–16)

There are more shocks! First the vineyard owner calls the worker who confronts him "friend." Then he says something about himself — that he chooses to treat all of the workers equally and pay them all the same. This is his justice. And he tells the worker that he's getting paid what he is because that was the deal they had made earlier, and he honors his commitments. Then he chastises the worker, however gently, telling him to be content and go home. The vineyard owner is who he is. He is generous and will continue to be generous even if offends others, such as those who judge their own lives and relationships against their own standards of what they perceive to be others' good fortune. Their standard breeds enviousness and society built on competition between winners and losers.

Then Jesus repeats one of his signature lines: "Thus the last will be first, and the first, last." Unlike in the kingdoms of the world, in the kingdom of heaven things work differently — fortune, power, even position. This, one of Jesus' most difficult parables, reveals most clearly his vision, his wisdom, the coming of the kingdom of heaven on earth. The kingdom comes in his presence and in the hope and good news that God is our Father and we are the children of God — different only in our different needs, the neediest coming first.

The above parable's meaning and depth can be found by examining the description of how workers are chosen. When the owner comes out at the eleventh hour and sees workers standing around he asks them why they are idle. Their answer provides a key to understanding the true meaning of the parable: "No one has hired us." They are the ones no one wants, no one invites in, no one thinks to have work for — they are the least of our brothers and sisters. If the vineyard owner was interested only in getting his grapes picked efficiently and quickly, he would choose the best, the able-bodied, the experienced, the strong and healthy. Only later would he take the second best, then whoever might be able to work for a while, and then as the day goes he might choose the least — disabled, sick, ill, old, young children with little or no experience, or those thought to be slackers and trouble-makers. But this owner is interested not in productivity, but in making sure everyone is included. Jesus' parable reminds us that everyone needs food, shelter, health care, whatever gives a human being dignity, not mere survival but life ever more abundant.

In the kingdom of heaven God is concerned first with those at the bottom, those never chosen or chosen last, and so it must be with us. We are called to forgiveness, to reconciliation (walking with each other in all situations) and we are called to at-one-ment. It means all being one in the community and treated and respected as the beloved children of God, but also singling out those who are last, lost, not chosen, despised and forgotten, the least, to be honored first, cared for first. This is atonement. This is the beginning of restoring the world. It is the beginning, as the Jews call it, *oftikkum olam* — repairing the world. We are to extend the gracious experience of forgiveness and reconciliation to those who have never known justice, equality, or dignity, who have never realized that they are the beloved children of God. We are all the brothers and sisters of Jesus — we are all one in our God.

In the parable those who worked and came first (like the chosen people of the earlier covenant) do not deal with the foreman who pays them, but they take their complaint straight to the vineyard owner. But Jesus changes the way God is known and revealed in the world — in obedience to his knowledge of God as our Father. The parable hints at what is to come. Those who came first, and some of those who want the older covenant and the older interpretation of the laws and traditions to prevail, reject the foreman, Jesus, as well as his message that professing belief in God our Father, depends upon this new mercy, this new awareness and care for the least. Through this parable, Jesus is teaching that in the kingdom of heaven, so "close at hand," those closest and nearest to God — the poor and the lost, those most in need, those excluded by others — are the ones who reveal the presence of God so close to us. We touch God most intimately and closely in those shunned by society and even by church, by our own communities.

We are called to extend to them forgiveness and reconciliation into communion, into unity. This community of the kingdom of heaven, the presence of Jesus among us, and the power of the Spirit that gives glory to God the Father witnesses most strongly to others that God is with us. There is no limit to the depth and intimacy of what community can teach us about the pity, the compassion, the justice, and the holiness of our God.

The culmination of understanding forgiveness, reconciliation and at-one-ment is communion among us and, if we learn from Jesus how to "walk together again," among all on earth. This is God the Father's gift to us in Jesus and in the Spirit — communion with God.

I would like to close with a story I heard a few months after 9/11.

* A group had gone to visit the Acoma Pueblo, on a high mesa just east of Albuquerque. Its residents, who still honor the old ways and traditions, call it Sky City. After their tour of the pueblo, some of the visitors lingered to buy the pottery or bread that some of the Sky City community were selling. They began to talk to one of the elders sitting in front of his house about the events of 9/11. They asked him, "How did you hear about the news that day?" He answered, "We found out just like you did," and pulled out his cell phone. Everyone laughed because there is no running water or electricity up on the top of the mesa. Then the elder grew silent and looked at the group, all of whom were intently listening to him now. He said: "I'm so sorry. I apologize. It was our fault. It was all our fault." No

one knew what the man meant, or how to respond. He realized they did not understand him, so he said again: "I am so sorry. We all are. It was — it is our fault. You see, we believe that we are all one. We have a saying that is sometimes translated as 'all our relations' — it means that we are all one — everything and everyone created: birds, fish, animals, four-leggeds, two-leggeds, all human beings everywhere in the world. And we are responsible for each other and what others do. So it is our fault. We have not lived as we should. If we were living as human beings, other human beings would not be driven to do such terrible things. They would not be without hope, and filled with so much despair. We are so sorry, please forgive us. It is our fault that it happened." His words left everyone in the group speechless, and they wandered off awkwardly to buy their fry bread or pottery, and to walk or take their tour bus back down the mesa.

When I heard it, the story made perfect sense to me. We must honor all our relations so that something as horrible as 9/11 can never happen again. This is the culmination of understanding forgiveness, reconciliation and at-one-ment. It is communion among us and among all on earth — this is God the Father's gift to us in Jesus and in the Spirit — communion with God.

Questions

1. What sin do you think is the hardest to forgive? Why? Do you think this sin is worse than others you can commit? Why? If you refuse to forgive an individual, or a group, what do you think Jesus expects you to do?

2. Do you demand more from some people than others? Why? Are there people who you consider beyond forgiveness? Why?

3. How do you think Jesus would approach people considered "public sinners" in the church today? What can we do to practice reconciliation and atonement with others, without condemnation, keeping the doors open for all to return?

7

Healings and Feedings

There is a story from the early church (between the late second and the sixth centuries A.D.) that was told among the brothers and sisters who gathered in the desert to become holy, once the age of martyrdom had passed:

> * Two brothers lived in the desert. Each had his own cell and followed the order of the prayers, study, fasting, and work. One rarely ventured out his cell, praying and fasting and doing penance for his sins and the sins of the world. The other followed the order of the night and day but rarely stayed in his cell. He went out daily, even on the day of the Son, to seek the sick and to bring them water, to bathe and clean them, and to tend their wounds, to feed them and comfort them. He would stay and listen to them, touch them carefully, sometimes be silent and sometimes sing to them. And an Elder who had been in the desert longest was asked: which of the two brothers is the most holy?
>
> Without hesitation he replied: "If the brother who fasts and prays were to do this for seventy years and endure all manner of hardships in silence, and suffer terrible penances — his whole life would not equal even one moment of kindness and care of the brother who cares for the sick and the infirm. You have to ask? How long have you been among us and do not know this truth?"

This strong story contradicts a great deal of what has come to be seen over the centuries as spirituality and the basis of holiness, yet it surely echoes what Jesus himself does in his life with his disciples. Along with Jesus' preaching and teaching, even his confrontations with others, his healings of and his relationships with those who are sick and suffering, whether from disease or from others' condemnation of them, speak most clearly about the kingdom of heaven on earth — what it looks like and what it demands of those who dwell in it now.

Jesus begins his preaching with the message: "Repent, for the kingdom of heaven is at hand" (Mt 4:17). This proclamation is followed by Jesus' calling the first of his disciples and then, before he records Jesus' first sermon, Matthew accounts for what he does to reveal what this kingdom of heaven looks like now, here:

> He went around all of Galilee, teaching in their synagogues, proclaiming the gospel of the kingdom, and curing every disease and illness among the people. His fame spread to all of Syria, and they brought to him all who were sick with various diseases and racked with pain, those who were possessed, lunatics, and paralytics, and he cured them. And great crowds from Galilee, the Decapolis, Jerusalem, and Judea, and from beyond the Jordan followed him. (Mt 4:23–25)

Jesus' magnetic presence draws toward him anyone in pain, anyone suffering, and anyone in need of the kingdom of heaven that makes all people whole and so holy before God and among others in the world. In Matthew's Gospel those who are healed represent the groups that reveal God's presence and nearness to all the others, as well as remind the community that they must attend to individuals and groups who suffer first and continuously as witness to the presence of the kingdom of heaven. The healings start in chapter 8 with a leper, a centurion's servant, Peter's mother-in-law, the demoniacs in the neighborhood of Gadara, a paralytic, a woman with a hemorrhage, an official's daughter who dies before Jesus can reach her, two blind men, and a dumb demoniac. The numbers and the kinds of healings are staggering. The two chapters of healings end with a gathering of all the people — the masses and crowds — all of whom need Jesus' preaching, touch, and presence:

> Jesus went around to all the towns and villages, teaching in their synagogues, proclaiming the gospel of the kingdom, and curing every disease and illness. At the sight of the crowds, his heart was moved with pity for them because they were troubled and abandoned, like sheep without a shepherd. Then he said to his disciples, "The harvest is abundant but the laborers are few, so ask the master of the harvest to send out laborers for his harvest." (Mt 9:35–38)

Everyone needs healing, hope, and inclusion. And the world needs those who will follow Jesus' way of being a good shepherd, who keeps healthy and gathers in those entrusted to him, providing them water, food, shelter, protection. This shepherd is not merely a symbolic figure, but someone who supplies the basic necessities of life. Even though there are so many healings, we will examine a number of them specifically because they focus on issues of community life and priorities as well as revelations essential to Matthew's sense of identity for the community. Even though it is short, the first, the healing of the leper, reveals where the power of healing lies in Jesus:

> And then a leper approached, did him homage, and said, "Lord, if you wish, you can make me clean." He stretched out his hand, touched him, and said, "I will do it. Be made clean." His leprosy was cleansed immediately. Then Jesus said to him, "See that you tell no one, but go show yourself to the priest, and offer the gift that Moses prescribed; that will be proof for them." (Mt 8:2–4)

The healing reveals many issues: Jesus' intent and will, how he heals, the relationship between healed and healer, and the larger issue of community and how healing is connected to forgiveness, reconciliation with the community, and the unity of the community — despite the religious leadership that controls ritual and life. And it is a leper — the most excluded and feared of those who are sick.

Even someone like this, who was blamed for his illnesses by others, especially by the religious leaders, could be healed and allowed back into the community and the ritual life of the people. Lepers were untouchable — whoever touched them disobeyed both tradition and religious law, and were subsequently treated as lepers as well. Lepers were shunned and were manipulated to control the larger community. Only the power and the authority of the priests could return the leper to life, acceptance, and normal status within society.

Clearly, Jesus wills the healing, the making whole, and the inclusion of others back into life, commerce, and relationship. Jesus not only stretches out his hand and touches the leper, he says: "I do will it!" This is the will of God for all — life shared and experienced with others, no matter what, and life ever more abundant that makes us all more human, especially when we are in need and painfully aware of our lack, our failure, our sickness and our repugnancy. Jesus asked him not to tell others out of self-protection. To touch a leper made you as unclean as the one proscribed according to the law — and yet Jesus tells him to go and offer the traditional sacrifice, honor the old ways, and present himself to the authorities so that he could be declared safe and clean once again, and rejoin ordinary life. No one is to be treated badly, scorned, or called a leper, not in Jesus' community or in the kingdom of heaven. We still proscribe people today: those with diseases that terrify us and so are considered unclean or unworthy of participation in ritual or common society, those who have committed certain sins or who take stands to minister to those excluded or labeled unfit to sit at the table of the Lord. And yet these are the first that Jesus welcomes into the kingdom and embraces wholeheartedly as a call for us to imitate and follow. This is the first step in making the kingdom, the community, and the church whole.

The next story, the healing of the centurion's servant, also involves an outsider, an enemy of the Jewish community and a member of the Roman legion that occupied Israel. But it seems Jesus excludes no one from the wholeness of the circle of God's children. He ignores no one's pain or grief:

When he entered Capernaum, a centurion approached him and appealed to him, saying, "Lord, my servant is lying at home paralyzed, suffering dreadfully." He said to him, "I will come and cure him." The centurion said in reply, "Lord, I am not worthy to have you enter under my roof; only say the word and my servant will be healed. For I too am a person subject to authority, with soldiers subject to me. And I say to one, 'Go,' and he goes; and to another, 'Come here,' and he comes; and to my slave, 'Do this,' and he does it." When Jesus heard this, he was amazed and said to those following him. "Amen, I say to you, in no one in Israel have I found such faith. I say to you, many will come from the east and the west and will recline with Abraham, Isaac, and Jacob at the banquet in the kingdom of heaven, but the children of the kingdom will be driven out into the outer darkness, where there will be wailing and grinding of teeth. And Jesus said to the centurion, "You may go; as you have believed, let it be done for you." And at that very hour [his] servant was healed. (Mt 8:5–13)

This story introduces a number of new elements: the centurion's faith based on his own lived experience that he transfers to his relationship with Jesus; the amazement that he gives Jesus — delighting him and yet causing Jesus to contrast the faith of outsiders, pagans, even enemies to those who should have been open to his words, his touch, and his presence. The banquet feast he alludes to is the ritual celebration of the ingathering of all the lost — the outcast, strangers, those newly come to the kingdom after having known Jesus' care and concern for them. The Roman soldier, an officer, recognizes Jesus' authority and power and so realizes that the power of the empire, the power of Rome, is nothing in relation to Jesus' own person — he is not worthy to have Jesus enter his own home and Rome is not worthy or even aware of the power and authority that is in its midst. The authority to stop suffering, to alleviate pain, to make whole, to heal paralysis, to affect even those at a distance and to bring together those who oppose one another — these powers belie the false power of dominant nations — destruction, mutilation, paralysis, long hatreds, mass murder, indiscriminate attacks and killing, maiming, destruction of water, food, and health facilities. No nation can long stand against the power of Jesus, who brings hope, healing, and feasting with others here on earth now. Matthew begins with stories of those far from the community and works his way toward stories about the believers themselves. The third, probably the shortest healing story in the text, occurs closer to home. It too is again layered with intent, meaning and consequences:

> Jesus entered the house of Peter, and saw his mother-in-law lying in bed with a fever. He touched her hand, the fever left her, and she rose and waited on them. (Mt 8:14–15)

Jesus visits Peter's house and Peter's mother-in-law, so Peter is married. But no mention is made of his wife or children. Traditionally, their not being mentioned means they are dead or they were not believers. But Peter cares for his mother-in-law. He goes beyond the law, drawing in someone that he was not required to care for, if his wife is dead (the usual cause of death was childbirth). And Jesus goes to her and touches her — no words, just grasps her by the hand, the usual way of touching someone who is sick in bed. The description of the healing is staccato — seeing, touch, fever leaves, she rises and waits on him. It is the story of a member of the community who encounters Jesus, is touched by him body and soul, and her response is resurrection — rising up to new life, new relationships, and new connections to others.

And she "waited on him." This is the same word the text uses elsewhere to describe a deacon, waiting at the table of the Lord — Eucharist — and feeding those in need. At this point, Matthew has named only four disciples: Simon, Andrew, James, and John — the two sets of brothers. Now there is another — Peter's mother-in-law, who becomes a disciple, a follower of Jesus in gratitude for Jesus' taking her hand and bringing her life that is stronger than fever, weakness, or anything else that threatens the fullness of life. This, of course, is the life response for anyone in Matthew's community who has been touched, healed, forgiven by Jesus — a lifetime of service and discipleship — and it is to be the same among us. The only way to thank the one who

heals us and gives us life is to live in gratitude, to do Eucharist together
and to care for the others who are the Body of Christ. The community
is coming together — formed of sinners, the sick, the shunned,
servants, and even centurions and Romans.

This short introduction to healing ends with Matthew once again
connecting Jesus' words and actions with the tradition of the prophets
who announced the coming of the anointed one of God:

> When it was evening, they brought him many who were
> possessed by demons, and he drove out the spirits by a word
> and cured all the sick, to fulfill what had been said by Isaiah
> the prophet:
> "He took away our infirmities and bore our diseases."
> (Mt 8:16–17)

Jesus heals with his word, the word of the gospel that calls all to
repentance, to a life of truthfulness, integrity, awareness of others and
homage to God, along with study of the scripture and shared life, food,
and future. Jesus heals with the word of the gospel that is forgiveness,
mercy, and being at home once again with God and all our brothers and
sisters. Jesus heals with his touch and his presence and — startlingly
— he bears our diseases, our lack, our sin, our illnesses, our failures,
our incompleteness, even the inhumanity that we ourselves experience
and that we inflict upon others. What Jesus does echoes the passion of
the prophets and intimates the passion that will come upon him
because he touches the sinner, embraces and eats with those who
society and religion condemn as unworthy or evil. He bears our human
life of pain and yearning and need before he bears the cross of injustice,
torture, and rejection that will kill him. When he sided with the human
family, he sided with those considered expendable and those imprisoned as a result of others' disdain and hate. He came to draw us all into
the intimacy of the children of his beloved Father, in the power of the
reconciling and Holy Spirit.

In these passages, the word used to name what Jesus does is
"cure," and the centurion says ". . . my servant will be healed." These
words, "cure," and "heal" are connected to forgiving and reconciling. "Cure" carries the connotation of something over and done

with, something that will not reoccur. "Heal," on the other hand, suggests an ongoing process, including what has come before and what will come after. In a sense there is no cure for living — even those whom Jesus cures must eventually die — but we often, perhaps always, need healing. To heal is to restore to sound health, and health is the state of being whole. To heal, then, means to ease, to soothe, to enhance, to facilitate, and to give meaning to a life (body, soul, mind, and heart) beset by the disease, suffering, and pain that renders it not whole. Healing transforms illness and loss so that a person who lacks wholeness lives with enduring grace, not in spite of sickness but through it.

The afflicted — an individual or a community — needs more than a simple remedy or cancellation of pain. Since all of us will grow older, grow weak, suffer illness, and die, healing is core to living itself. Throughout the many seasons and circumstances of our lives, healing makes us whole, and so, holy. C. S. Lewis wrote: "God whispers to us in our pleasures, speaks in our conscience, but shouts in our pain: it is His megaphone to rouse a deaf world."[1] And this could be said of the experience not only for individuals, but also for the community. Pain and illness make us acknowledge our dependence on others and place us before our own mortality, and so, before the presence of God.

Throughout history, religion has sometimes blamed the sick and those with deformity or other shortcomings for their predicaments, adding to their pain. Even those born with such conditions have been shamed, isolated, and declared unclean and sinful, considered somehow deserving of their painful experience. Such judgment does not reflect the God of mercy, the tender regard and care of the one Jesus calls Father and exhorts us to call Our Father with him, in the grace of the Spirit. One healing story contrasts paralysis and disdain in the name of religion with the support of friends, condemnation of sickness with the healing power of forgiveness. It takes place in Jesus' own town, among those already set on rejecting Jesus because they think they know him:

---

1. *The Problem of Pain* (New York: Harper Collins, 2001), 91.

He entered a boat, made the crossing, and came into his own town. And there people brought to him a paralytic lying on a stretcher. When Jesus saw their faith, he said to the paralytic, "Courage, child, your sins are forgiven." At that, some of the scribes said to themselves, "This man is blaspheming." Jesus knew what they were thinking, and said, "Why do you harbor evil thoughts? Which is easier, to say, 'Your sins are forgiven,' or to say, 'Rise and walk'? But that you may know that the Son of Man has authority on earth to forgive sins" — he then said to the paralytic, "Rise, pick up your stretcher, and go home." He rose and went home. When the crowds saw this they were struck with awe and glorified God who had given such authority to human beings. (Mt 9:1–8)

This story interlaces many relationships and levels of authority. The religious leaders, teachers, and scribes are sure they know how God operates — surely not through human beings, and not through Jesus. The story also demonstrates the authority of friendship, faith, and forgiveness, more powerful and transformative than any law or formula. Jesus confronts us, too, with his question: "Which is easier to say [and therefore to make reality], 'Your sins are forgiven,' or ... 'Rise and walk'?" Reflect before you answer, remembering what forgiveness is and what it entails for the one who forgives and what its consequences are for the one forgiven and brought home, embraced once again, and pulled back together with everyone else. I was once preaching during a parish mission and when this scripture passage came up, I asked that question of the community. After a long, awkward silence in the huge church, a child, perhaps six or seven years old, called out, "It's easier to say get up and walk!" Everyone laughed. When I asked him why he said that, he stood up and said, "It's so hard to forgive. I have three sisters all older than me and I know!" Again there was a roar of laughter and then silence — this time, quiet, reflective silence as the truth hit home.

How interconnected within the most intimate part of our selves, body and soul, are the realities of sin and the need to be forgiven, and sickness, depression, despair, isolation, and general disease? The profound need to be accepted, to belong, to be whole, to be with others, and to be given another chance at holiness and life ever more abundant is part of every illness, sickness, accident, and even psychological disorder. In the story the paralytic's friends carry him physically into the presence of Jesus. It is their friendship in the face of rejection that Jesus sees and that precipitates the healing and the forgiveness he proclaims aloud so all can hear it, actions and words that welcome the man and draw him back into life and society.

Some of the religious leaders in this story take no delight in someone being brought back into the community. They see only an authority that threatens their range of influence. They do not seem to care that the man suffers physically or that his own family and neighbors, who perhaps think that he deserves his suffering, have shunned him. These scribes are concerned only that someone has contradicted them and their teaching, so they accuse Jesus of blasphemy, of appropriating to himself powers that belong only to God (though carefully regulated through their own interpretations, pronouncements, and rituals). And for Jesus, that in itself is a sickness that he will not let go unacknowledged even in public. He confronts their hardened hearts that would will to continue perpetrating the pain and exclusion rather than to rejoice in God's forgiveness and gift of life. When Jesus speaks the paralytic, the one who cannot move or walk, rises up to return to his home, his life, his loved ones and his future. He goes in hope with the healing of Jesus. Who in the story do we stand with? Do we, as Matthew's community was being exhorted to do, stand with the sick and those incapable of taking care of themselves, and carry them into the presence of Jesus, into the kingdom of justice and peace? Or do we stand with the crowds who might be amazed by the miracle but don't move to follow Jesus? Or do we stand with those who condemn rather than care for those who suffer not only from disease but from judgment, even derision, by the community and its leaders? We are called to stand with Jesus, proclaiming God's forgiveness and healing power, to bring hope, to bring people home to life and a future lived in the power of Jesus' Word and presence in the community.

This story is about so much more than the curing of a physical ailment. Like the entire chapter from which it is taken, it is about who is sick and who needs forgiveness. It is about those who reject Jesus and his words outright, and those who respond truthfully, repent, and follow his new way of life. One motif runs through all of these stories — Jesus' depth and breath of compassion for all. In the very next paragraph Jesus calls a minor tax collector, Matthew, to be one of his disciples and then goes to Matthew's house to eat with him and his friends — in startling defiance of the cultural and religious taboos of Jewish society at that time:

> While he was at table in his house, many tax collectors and sinners came and sat with Jesus and his disciples. The Pharisees saw this and said to his disciples, "Why does your teacher eat with tax collectors and sinners?" He heard this and said, "Those who are well do not need a physician, but the sick do. Go and learn the meaning of the words, 'I desire mercy, not sacrifice.' I did not come to call the righteous but sinners." (Mt 9:10–13)

The Pharisees, whose job it was to gather and hold the people of God together, refuse to deal with Jesus directly. But Jesus is blunt. He is here for those who will admit that they are sick, that they are sinners, that they need the mercy of God, that they need Jesus' ministrations and healing words and presence, but the Pharisees refuse to admit those things. He is teaching at every moment. He sits at table and eats with sinners and who he eats with lies at the heart of our religion — the Eucharist. The meal we share with Jesus, with one another at the table of the Lord, brings about the forgiveness of all sin and puts us in communion with our Father in the authority and power of the Spirit, and so makes us one with everyone else as well. This is the Good News, the mercy that God gives us and wants us to give others. But we must begin by including ourselves with all those sinners who need God's mercy and his presence with us in Jesus. If we assume that others are not welcome at the table we might find ourselves not eating with Jesus in the kingdom of heaven.

Jesus never ceases to heal the sick, to make them whole, and to welcome them into his community. Some may continue to assign blame to those whom they call sinners, and refuse to admit them to religious rituals, but by doing so they resist Jesus' proclamation of God as a Father who is merciful and forgiving if we forgive, but just if we do. Disputing theological interpretations of minute laws having to do with Sabbath practice with the leaders, Jesus repeats: "If you knew what this meant, 'I desire mercy, not sacrifice,' you would not have condemned these innocent men. For the Son of Man is Lord of the Sabbath" (Mt 12:7–8). The religious leaders refuse to listen and to heed Jesus' command: learn mercy! This is how we begin the process of healing among ourselves, in our relationships with each other, and to arrive at awareness of and gratefulness for God's mercy toward us.

Doug Lipman has developed a contemporary Jewish story based on an event in the life of the Baal Shem Tov, renowned as a teacher, healer, and a wise and compassionate human being.[2] This is how I tell it:

   * There once was a man with a seriously infected leg who went to the local physician. Just the next day, the doctor met him in the street and sternly told him that he was disobeying the doctor's rules not to walk for days, and to rest or else the infection would get even worse. His patient told him, "It is healed. I went to see the Baal Shem Tov, our holy rabbi, and he healed me. See, I can walk and there is little or no pain." The doctor was not happy — who was this healer? He'd heard of the rabbi before — many of the people in their ignorance went to him or any other person who claimed to heal, as well as coming to a real physician.

   So the doctor decided to pay this rabbi a visit. He found where he lived and banged on his door. Immediately, as though the doctor was expected, the door opened and the Baal Shem Tov appeared, smiling, and asked, "Yes, what can I do

---

2. http://www.hasidicstories.com/Stories/The_Baal_Shem_Tov/doctor.html.

for you? How can I be of service?" But the doctor was curt. "You think you're a healer? Leave my patients alone so that they might actually get better. What do you know of healing?" The Baal Shem Tov was not put out. He smiled, saying, "Please come into my house so that we can talk instead of standing in the doorway. Oh, I don't heal anyone. If anyone is healed, it is God who does the healing, not me." And so the doctor was pulled inside the house, but still he was not going to be taken in by this fake healer.

He made a proposal to the rabbi. "I will examine you and you can examine me. Let's see if we can diagnose what is wrong with each other and then we'll know who is the real doctor."

"Oh, all right. You can examine me first," said the Baal Shem Tov. And so the doctor started his examination and was very thorough: poking, prodding, asking for responses, testing reflexes, questioning the rabbi's diet and exercise, looking into his eyes, nose, ears, mouth. He took forever, examining every inch of the rabbi. Finally his offered his diagnosis. "There is absolutely nothing wrong with you at all. In fact you are in remarkably good shape for your age and how you live."

The Baal Shem Tov looked at him sadly and said, "I'm so sorry you could not see what is wrong with me. You see, I am in constant pain and I will surely die of my suffering." The doctor was frightened and the rabbi continued, "You see, I so desire the presence and knowledge of my God that I can barely stand it. It hurts so when I am not aware of God's nearness. I suffer terribly because I want and need to obey and serve God." Then he stood silent, looking at the doctor.

After a while, the doctor coughed and said, "Very well, now you examine me and see if there is anything wrong with me. Begin your examination." The Baal Shem Tov kept looking at him, hard, yet kindly, sadly and then moved in closer and took both of the doctor's hands into his own. He just stood, holding them, looking at him. Finally he spoke. "I'm so sorry. You have lost something so valuable." Visibly shaken, the doctor answered, "How could you know? It was so recent. I was robbed and something I treasured, a stone of great value, given to me by a loved one, was taken. I have been so distraught over losing it. It is irreplaceable." The Baal Shem Tov said softly, "Yes, I know this is your disease."

"What? What are you talking about? I was robbed."

Again the rabbi spoke softly, "My sickness is that I long for God and my heart is breaking. Your sickness is that you've lost your longing for God and you don't even your how sick unto death already you really are."

Struck dumb, the doctor couldn't respond. And then he began to cry, first a tear or two and then uncontrollable weeping, shaking and sobbing like a young child. The Baal Shem Tov held onto him, taking him into his embrace until the doctor's sobs finally stopped. Then the rabbi looked at him again and smiled broadly. "Ah, your healing has begun already. Look into your heart, feel the pain, the ache rising up again." He walked the doctor to the door with his arm around his shoulders. "Now, to continue your healing and speed it up immensely, look at those who come to you, hold their hands, feel their sufferings and let it feed the desire in your own heart. And whenever you are moved to tears, weep in gratitude. It will cleanse and open your eyes. Come back whenever you wish — you are always welcome here."

This story is directed at and about each of us. We have physical sicknesses and social ills and incurable diseases and lacks and aches and pains deeper and stronger and sometimes more destructive and deadly than any bodily pain. Jesus is intent on making us holy, making us whole, in communion with one another and with God our Father, on "inspiriting" us so that we are the presence of God, the presence of healing and mercy in the world. And he is most intent on opening our eyes, washing them out along with our hearts so that we can see others' need and respond compassionately instead of judging them and condemning or being condescending to them. He weaves together diverse issues: the practice of the law, obedience to

God in worship and in honoring the Sabbath, and compassion toward everyone, making whole the way we live our lives, body, soul, mind, and heart. He keeps trying to teach those who, revealing their own inhumanity and sinfulness, find this all too demanding. He keeps trying to teach all of us:

> Moving on from there, he went into their synagogue. And behold, there was a man who had a withered hand. They questioned him, "Is it lawful to cure on the Sabbath?" so they might accuse him. He said to them, "Which one of you who has a sheep that falls into a pit on the Sabbath will not take hold of it and lift it out? How much more valuable a person is than a sheep. So it is lawful to do good on the Sabbath." Then he said to the man, "Stretch out your hand." He stretched it out, and it was restored as sound as the other. But the Pharisees went out and took counsel against him to put him to death. (Mt 12:9–14)

God is not interested in our slavishly keeping laws, or following correct ritual. God is interested in our stretching out our hands to one another and restoring people to health and community. God is interested in stretching our hearts that at our baptisms have been given the mercy and forgiveness of God, along with the healing holy presence of the Spirit of God with Jesus. Jesus is making the three imperatives of the prophets into one: to worship God with integrity and truthfulness is to care for the least and those among us in most need and pain, and that brings the kingdom of justice and abiding peace upon the earth. Worshipping God cannot be separated from how we treat one another and how we practice the corporal and spiritual works of mercy, how we learn to be compassionate like Our Father is compassionate. We have Jesus' own practices to imitate and incorporate into our lives as believers and as church.

Just as during the time of Jesus and in Matthew's own community some quarreled and quibbled over details of liturgy and law instead of stretching out their hands in faith, in forgiveness, and in mercy to those who were excluded and judged, so it is with us today. Then as now, there are the many, the masses of people desperate for Jesus' touch, even if it is the fringe of his clothes, desperate for his presence because they know their sin, their pain, and their longing for God. As the gospel continues, the crowds continue to seek out Jesus:

> After making the crossing, they came to land at Gennesaret. When the men of that place recognized him, they sent word out to all the surrounding country. People brought to him all whose who were sick, and begged him that they might touch only the tassel on his cloak, and as many as touched it were healed. (Mt 14:34–36)

"As many as touched ... were healed" is a refrain throughout the gospel. People seek to reach out for him in their need, and Jesus lets himself be touched. Again and again Matthew's community is urged to stretch out their hands, their hearts, and imitate Jesus, remembering their own need and how they have been drawn close to God in Jesus' words, in meals, in the way their lives have changed. Matthew's community become the very tassels of Jesus' cloak that draw people close to God and bring them to Jesus. The whole world is seeking healing, and we who have experienced it must share it generously, continuously, as did Jesus.

One final healing is a benchmark, a turning point in Matthew's Gospel. Jesus has been teaching, interpreting the law, in dialogue and discussion, even in heated exchanges with the teachers, the scribes and Pharisees. More and more, however, they block any real communication with him. Time and again, they reject him. More than half-way through Matthew's Gospel we find the healing of the Canaanite woman's daughter:

> Then Jesus went from that place and withdrew to the region of Tyre and Sidon. And behold, a Canaanite woman of that district came and called out, "Have pity on me, Lord, Son of David! My daughter is tormented by a demon." But he did not say a word in answer to her. His disciples came and asked him, "Send her away, for she keeps calling after us." He said in reply, "I was sent only to the lost sheep of the house of Israel." But the woman came and did him homage,

saying, "Lord, help me." He said in reply, "It is not right to
take the food of the children and throw it to the dogs." She
said, "Please, Lord, for even the dogs eat the scraps that fall
from the table of their masters." Then Jesus said to her in
reply, "O woman, great is your faith! Let it be done for you
as you wish." And her daughter was healed from that hour.
(Mt 15:21–28)

Rejected by his own people, their leaders, his own town, and
even his own family, Jesus withdraws outside Israel to cities of
the pagans, of nonbelievers. The woman who comes to him is a
Canaanite, a descendant of the original residents of the promised
land. He has healed many, forgiven and shared meals and hope with
many of his own land and religion, but few have taken anything he
has said or done to heart. Now Jesus is the outsider, the stranger in
another land, and he is trying to be inconspicuous and lie low.

But the woman is desperate on behalf of her child — even more
than the Roman centurion who came to Jesus on behalf of his servant.
She aches for her child who is so tormented by a demon — that is, any
disease or affliction that did not seem to have any natural cause. It
usually meant an inability to control one's body, or behavior that was
self-destructive or dangerous to others — what we would diagnose
today as anything from advanced Alzheimer's to epilepsy, seizures,
mental illness, behaviors after strokes or during high fevers, encepha-
litis, and so forth. She pursues Jesus loudly and persistently, and she
honors him with the title "Lord, Son of David" — a title that his own
people deny him. Horrified and without compassion, his own disciples
want her to go away. They want Jesus to get rid of her because she's
making a scene. Troubled already by their own people's rejection of
Jesus, they are confused and concerned about their own presence in
another country. They have been with Jesus so long, yet it seems his
compassion has not rubbed off on them.

Jesus' behavior may strike us as strange because it doesn't match
the perceptions that we overlay on Jesus' actual person, making him
divine but not really human. He is escaping from harsh realities —
rejection, disillusionment, discouragement, sadness, frustration, and

weariness. He does not respond to her cries immediately, but neither does he respond to his disciples' callousness. But she keeps after him; she won't be ignored. What Jesus says to her is perfectly true and obvious: he is a Jew, a Jewish teacher, preacher, and prophet and his words, his actions, his life are dedicated not to outsiders, to pagans and unbelievers, but to his own people, Israel. He describes himself as he has before, and as Matthew often describes him: a shepherd who knows his own sheep and cares only for them. "I was sent only to the lost sheep of the house of Israel." This is Matthew's representation of Jesus' self-awareness as a prophet and as the Beloved servant of Israel's God Yahweh, who Jesus knows as Our Father.

The woman does him homage, as did the Magi from the East, as also do many others who acknowledge him as more than a teacher in Israel. To "do homage" would have meant approaching him on her knees, bending to the ground before him as she pleads piteously. Jesus again uses an image that captures the way people in Israel and those outside Israel actually thought of each other, spoke about each other, and disdained each others' presence. The law, for example, required that Jews not eat with Gentiles. This too is an issue in Matthew's own community, a mix of Jews and Gentiles struggling to replace old laws and traditions with the new way of Jesus, including eating regularly with people whom the law proscribed. Jesus has been giving the food of the gospel to the children of Israel, and the woman describes accurately what those children have been doing with that food: they have been throwing it away, not realizing or respecting what is being given to them. What she says rings true to Jesus: "Please, Lord, for even the dogs eat the scraps that fall from the table of their masters." To us it sounds awful, demeaning, insulting, but at the time it reveals the woman's deep love for her child, her desperation to find relief for her daughter, and her under-standing that Jesus belongs to all people, not just to the children of Israel. Like so many others, she will take what those children reject and embrace it; she does homage to Jesus and believes in him. This is the experience of many pagans who have come to believe in Jesus and are baptized in Matthew's struggling church.

Heartened by her faith, Jesus responds! Her daughter is healed, and Jesus himself shifts base, turning from feeding only the children of Israel to feeding anyone and everyone who is hungry. Except for a passage very late in the gospel when he cures two blind men as he comes out of Jericho, and then his healing the severed ear of the high priest's servant in the garden when he is arrested, this is the last story of Jesus performing a specific healing. The healings have covered every kind of lack: muteness, deafness, blindness, paralysis, illness. All are more than merely physical; they reveal the deeper sickness of not being able to see Jesus for who he is; not hearing the Word of God; not praying and speaking on behalf of others; not acting on what has been heard, and succumbing to the despair and illnesses of the world and its practices in relation to others. These healings are intended to be calls to faith, to belief and the practice of hope, justice, and compassion that effect radical change and repentance in our own hearts, minds, spirits, and bodies, and in those of others around us. Jesus takes leave of the Canaanite woman who reveals to him who he actually is — God's Word for all peoples reaching out to everyone:

> Moving on from there Jesus walked by the Sea of Galilee, went up the mountain, and sat down there. Great crowds came to him, having with them the lame, the blind, the deformed, the mute, and many others. They placed them at his feet, and he cured them. The crowds were amazed when they saw the mute speaking, the deformed made whole, the lame walking, and the blind able to see, and they glorified the God of Israel. (Mt 15:29–31)

Jesus will continue to preach and teach in Israel, but now he turns toward the whole world, offering his forgiveness and the gospel and the kingdom of heaven on earth to all. With this story a door opens from Israel offering its earlier testament and covenants to the world at large. The story of feeding the five thousand (chapter 14) precedes it, and just afterwards Matthew places the story of feeding the four thousand. In the ritual of feeding crowds that need and seek holiness and God in Jesus, we see the connection between healing and wholeness, between forgiveness and breaking and sharing bread together in the community with Jesus — the making of communion between us and God, and with each other.

After he feeds the five thousand, Jesus withdraws "up on the mountain by himself to pray" (Mt 14:23), without his disciples. Herod has had John the Baptist beheaded, and Jesus must pray and reflect on the brutality of his own people's leaders, knowing that his cousin has trod the path of the prophets and that he too, if he moves publicly now, will go the same way. Afterwards, in the well-known incident when he walks on water (Mt 14: 26–34), Jesus joins his disciples who have been crossing the sea by boat, but the people follow him on land. Jesus will move into an even more public aspect of his preaching, healing, and authority among the people as a prophet who replaces John the Baptist, but he is so much more than a prophet. Even though he is weighted down with the reality of institutional violence as evidenced in John's murder, Jesus is moved with compassion for the mass of people who must deal every day with the consequences of such evil:

> When he disembarked and saw the vast crowd, his heart was moved with pity for them, and he cured their sick. When it was evening, the disciples approached and said, "This is a deserted place and it is already late; dismiss the crowds so that they can go to the villages and buy food for themselves." (Jesus) said to them, "There is no need for them to go away; give them some food yourselves." (Mt 14:14–16)

The disciples, who seem to want Jesus only to themselves, lack the pity that Jesus has for the people. His telling them to "give them some food yourselves" can be taken in a number of ways: give them food that you have. Give them yourselves, for they have been feeding on the Word of God and Jesus' presence for months, so don't expect that they feed themselves. The disciples respond by telling Jesus the amount of food they have: five loaves and two fish. He speaks curtly to his disciples: "Bring them here to me," and he orders the vast crowd to sit down on the grass — "orders" in the sense of giving them a command, but also in the sense of putting them in order since they were scattered physically across that deserted place, but also scattered internally, their hearts filled with fear and insecurity. Jesus performs a familiar ritual: he takes (from his own disciples); he looks to heaven and says the blessing (directed to God); he breaks the loaves; and he gives them to his disciples to distribute. This is Jesus' whole life: taking all that was given by God, blessing God, sharing everything that is God's, and seeking that those who follow him imitate him by sharing and giving as God gives: beginning with presence, teaching, and healing, and feeding: the basic necessities to live with one another and to live with God.

All human beings need to eat — everyone, believer or unbeliever. And all have enough: they are satisfied. And all have shared, from the disciples who shared reluctantly to anyone in the crowd who had anything to contribute. Matthew is clear about this because of the depth of detail that he supplies. He counts what's left over: enough fragments to fill twelve wicker baskets, baskets brought by members of the crowd, not the disciples. He counts the size of the crowd: "five thousand men, not counting women and children." Those who estimate the size of crowds suggest that there were probably five or six women and children for every man, so Jesus actually fed not five thousand, but twenty five thousand to thirty thousand. As he teaches, interprets the law, takes people to deserted places, climbs mountains, Jesus is, like Moses, the liberator and the lawgiver of Israel.

Following his encounter with the Canaanite woman, Matthew shows Jesus climbing another mountain to teach and heal. Again, Jesus feeds another crowd, but some important details differ from the story of feeding the five thousand. As before, Jesus is moved with pity, now because the crowd has been with him for three days (an image of the Paschal Mystery of life, death, and resurrection for Jesus and the community baptized, confirmed, and given Eucharist together and made the Body of Christ). Jesus is concerned that they might collapse along the way — the way of the kingdom of heaven on earth, the way of forgiveness and mercy, the way of the cross. Even though the disciples just witnessed an almost identical situation on the other side of the lake, they have not yet learned how to respond. Because they are once again reluctant to attend to the crowd's needs, Jesus has to ask them, "How many loaves do you have?" They respond, "Seven ... and a few fish." Again Jesus orders the crowd to sit down, takes, gives thanks, breaks the loaves, and gives them to the disciples to give to the crowds.

Again all the people, four thousand men, not counting women and children, are satisfied and collect the leftovers, enough to fill up seven baskets. The number seven represents the completeness of God: when people bless God by sharing with others what they have been given, enough is left over to feed the whole world. It is all the people, not just the disciples, not just the four thousand men, who actually share their food and resources. It is all the people — who represent the larger church — who bring food and give it freely to everyone in the crowd, gathering what is left over for those not yet in the presence of Jesus, who are not yet part of this community that has heard the Good News and known the healing hope of Jesus in their lifetime (represented by the three days). And it is all the people who share their surplus with those in need in the name of the larger church. This is Matthew's community, in life, in society, doing what they do at liturgical ritual. What they do must be done in life if ritual is to have any meaning. Worship must include Jesus' teaching, the Word, and his presence that heals, touches, stretches out to include others and breaks open hearts, but it likewise must include the actual sharing of all that God gives to his beloved children. Like the disciples and leaders of the community, we are slow to learn that we need to look to those in need, those not counted, to see how to imitate Jesus.

All these stories from Matthew's Gospel are not only accounts of what happened, but templates for life. A contemporary story shows how the elements important to Matthew's community — forgiveness, healing, feeding, hope, and the ability to deal with crowds that face violence and desperation — can be lived today. In 1993, 26-year-old Amy Biehl went as a Fulbright scholar to help prepare the people of South Africa for their first ever multi-racial elections. Days before she was to return home, an angry mob surrounded her car, smashed the windows, dragged her out, hit her with a brick, stabbed her, and left her to die by the side of the road. Two months after her funeral in California, Amy's mother Linda, her father Peter, and her sisters and brothers went to South Africa, as Linda said, to "celebrate Amy's life." For ten days they learned about the country, the people, and the desperate situations of the demonstrators who took Amy's life. As they saw the lack of food, the slow starvation, the meager education, health care, and housing, Amy's family began to understand the vast misery that produced the rage that had enveloped her. Many of those Linda met shared her grief, and she began to be able to forgive.

Over time, the rest of the family did too. They decided to establish a foundation to fund programs that would change the daily life of the people for whom Amy had worked: health care, day care, AIDS treatment, a bakery. Two of Amy's killers, Easy Nofemela and Ntobeko Peni, were 21 and 18 at the time they committed their crime. After serving four of their eighteen year prison sentences they were released in 1998 on the recommendation of the Truth and Reconciliation Commission. The young men asked to meet with Linda to apologize for what they had done. Their prison experience led them to seek ways of giving other children a chance for a peaceful life now that the system of apartheid had been abolished. Linda shared with them that their lives had not ended, but had only begun. She befriended them, and hired them to work in the bakery. When her husband died, Linda moved to Cape Town and now works and lives with the people among whom her daughter died. In an interview she said, "Coming to South Africa has made it easier to deal with the loss. Here nearly everyone has a story that would make your heart break. Here I've discovered I am not the only one who has suffered."

Jesus, compassionate, healing, and forgiving, is intent on feeding us and making us as compassionate toward others as God is with us. This is our life, our liturgy, our meaning as believers — followers of Jesus — and a community that is church. Which is hardest: Forgiving? Healing? Feeding? All are incredibly hard, yet incredibly freeing and life-giving.

Questions

1. How do you deal with your own sickness and disease? How do you deal with loved ones being sick, in pain, and suffering?

2. Are there people whose pain you dismiss or who you think deserve their pain? Why? What do you think it would be like to be related to them, or love them, or call them friends? Would that change the way you feel about them and their suffering?

3. What challenges do you face in living a life of forgiveness and healing that proclaims you as belonging to the children of God, the brothers and sisters of Jesus? What can you do, by yourself and with others, to learn compassion and mercy?

4. Do you know the corporal and spiritual works of mercy? Taking one of them a month, practice them by yourself and with a group. Talk about the experiences, pray about what you learn, and ask for the gift of being compassionate as our God is merciful to us.

8
Jesus' Parables

We love stories. As soon as we hear the words, "Once upon a time ..." something in us surges and turns toward the storyteller. When we hear the words with which Jesus begins most of his stories, "The kingdom of heaven is like ..." our own hearts and minds must turn and listen, intent to obey so that Jesus' stories of God might come true in our lives and in our world. Jesus' preferred story genre is the parable. It's not an easy form to describe — it is best experienced. Perhaps it is best to listen to one and then try to speak about it. This parable actually happened!

* A friend of mine spent more than 48 years, from the 1940s through the 1980s, as a missionary in Africa. They were times of change — violence, revolution, and massive shifts of power. During WWII it was especially difficult to get materials — everything from petrol and parts for his jeep to religious education materials, posters, and books. But on one trip home to England he was given a whole set of posters that illustrated all the teachings in the catechism. The people loved the full color pictures, and he used them between Masses every Sunday morning to teach.

   One Sunday morning the topic was heaven, hell, and purgatory. My friend tacked up the posters around the front of the church so that everyone could see them and went on to explain about each of the three places and why you might end up in one of them or another. The people were fascinated, especially with purgatory and hell, because the posters depicted in lurid detail what would happen to you if you found yourself there. As he continued preaching about what you shouldn't do — or else — the people started murmuring among themselves. Then they began poking each other to look, giggling and trying to repress smiles, and then they started laughing out loud. The preacher was put out because they were not taking this seriously. It was important for their lives and the future of their souls. Finally, the priest asked one of the catechists what was so funny, but the man was laughing so hard with the tears running down his face that he could barely get the words out. "Father," he said, "look!" The priest did, but didn't see anything all that funny. "No! Look!" the catechist said. "The only people in purgatory and hell are white!" The priest was shocked, but it was true … and finally he too laughed — but had a lot to think and reflect upon later.

That's a parable. It begins with something very ordinary and then it takes a turn, a twist; reality does a flip. Suddenly you view reality and your own life and place in it from a totally different angle and a piece of truth is staring you in the face. I call them doorways into the kingdom. They are not just stories, but actual entrances into the kingdom of heaven here now on earth. Parables draw us into a heightened awareness and into the presence of God, so we know for awhile what it's like to dwell there. Then we are summoned to decide whether we will block the doorways for others, just visit on occasion, or stay. The parables are secret, hidden presences of the kingdom of heaven on earth now, and icons of the Good News, but like the preaching of Jesus, to get in or understand with any clarity or depth what is being proclaimed and what is happening, it is necessary to repent. Parables all begin with practical realities that those listening can recognize immediately. Yet they are laced with strange details that conflict with or contradict experience. They deal with contemporary issues such as economics, politics, violence, or other brutal realities, and they do not mince words — in fact the parable takes a definite side in every matter and declares, sometimes abruptly, on which side you will find God or whom God sides with in the matter at hand.

A parable expands our horizons and seeks to stretch our minds so that we see from the vantage point of God (often called wisdom), and at the same time subverts the dominant view held by those in power. The parable gives an experience of what it's actually like to live in the kingdom of God! It is a judgment that reveals our resistance to God — how our blindness and deafness make us reject the vision and the hope preached in the gospels. It also conceals the depth and power of God from those who can't or won't appreciate the kingdom because they won't repent or change their minds, their hearts, or their lives. Each parable is a demand for conversion. It says bluntly: choose now or else! In some ways it is a desperate measure, a last-ditch attempt to get people to hear and take to heart what is spoken and so turn to face the teller and become believers. To understand the parable's depth and layers of meaning, those who are listening are assumed to have an attitude of openness and a willingness to acknowledge their lacks, their failures, and their refusal to live in the ways that the parable proclaims as the truth of God among us. The parable hits us broadside, demolishing what we accept as normative. It is one of Jesus' best ways of giving his friends "the secrets of the kingdom." But the parable can be confusing; it's not an easy form of story to hear or to tell. And Jesus' disciples have troubles with these stories:

> The disciples approached him and said, "Why do you speak to them in parables?" He said to them in reply, "Because knowledge of the mysteries of the kingdom of heaven has been granted to you, but to them it has not been granted. To anyone who has, more will be given and he will grow rich; from anyone who has not, even what he has will be taken away. This is why I speak to them in parables, because 'they look but do not see and hear but do not listen or understand.' Isaiah's prophecy is fulfilled in them, which says:
> 'You shall indeed hear but not understand,
> you shall indeed look but never see.
> Gross is the heart of this people,
> they will hardly hear with their ears,

they have closed their eyes,
lest they see with their eyes
and hear with their ears
and understand with their hearts
and be converted and I heal them.'

"But blessed are your eyes, because they see and your
ears because they hear. Amen, I say to you, many prophets
and righteous people longed to see what you see but did not
see it, and to hear what you hear but did not hear it."
(Mt 13:10–18)

Jesus begins to tell parables and to "hide" the depth of his teaching
in them because so many do not take his parables to heart. They hear
but they do not listen — meaning they do not obey what they hear in
the stories and they refuse to believe in Jesus or to follow him. For
those who are open to the Word, the parable opens and such people slip
into the experience of God on earth in Jesus and are touched and
known by the power of the Spirit of God. Too many ignore the
wisdom, or want signs to prove what Jesus says is true, or question who
he is and why he does what he does. They continue to persist in their
ways, to do evil, and to stick to their old assumptions that more often
than not allow them to twist the teachings of the law and the prophets to
serve their own ends, letting them continue to blame others for their
situations, and allowing them self-righteously to act without compassion or justice. Many leaders continue to listen because the parables
fascinate them, but they are also hypocritically looking for ways to
discredit Jesus and arrest him. Any parable is like a "hot potato"
thrown from person to person — no one wants to hold onto it for long.
Even though it can burn, it is meant to be chewed over, swallowed,
digested and assimilated into one's body and soul. Many parables are
not easy to listen to nor to put into practice.

In this passage, Matthew is reminding his own community that they
have been blessed with belief and with the wisdom that many who
went before them in faith hungered and yearned for, but died without
ever hearing. They too must remember to appreciate the words, the
stories, and the teachings of Jesus as jewels, as seeds that if nurtured

grow with power and grace, and are meant to bear fruit continually in their lives. He uses a strange line to describe those who have come to see and to hear and to understand with their hearts — "to anyone who has, more will be given and he will grow rich." That is, they have been given the secrets of God, they have been given God in the person of Jesus, in the Spirit of God in their baptisms! Matthew is questioning them, and we question ourselves whether we are hearing, listening, and obeying, taking the parables to heart and making them the reality of our lives, or whether we have grown lax, mute, deaf, and hard-hearted in spite of the mysteries that we have been honored to receive.

The parables are the dreams of God's kingdom that has arrived in the world in the person and presence of Jesus. They are reflections of Jesus' prayer, Jesus' Word, and Jesus' reason for being baptized and living among us — they are the reasons why we are baptized and dwell in communities of his Body, held together by the Spirit of God. The parables are always about the work of the kingdom, about the work of living the new relationship of being the brothers and sisters of Jesus, the beloved children of God, and witnessing to God our Father through the power of the Spirit. They always address four major issues:

1. The restoration of justice for all on earth
2. The vindication and rights of the poor
3. A repudiation of violence and witness of peace, of love even unto death because of our being rooted in the resurrection, and
4. How the church and the kingdom of heaven live and work within the dominant, outside world of politics, economics, powers, and violence which, because it opposes all that Jesus stands for and preaches, confronts and persecutes his followers.

For many, Jesus' preaching and his presence in the world are dangerous — for those who disdain or seek to use religion for their own ends and agenda, or pick and choose which pieces of truth to use as criteria for judgment and condemnation, rather than for self-conversion. Following Jesus is dangerous, for his followers know they might well die as he died, defending the truth, witnessing to the forgiveness and mercy of God as the only power to be recognized and obeyed on earth. A Chinese parable illustrates the telling of parables and making them come true in obedience to Jesus' words. It's called "Untying the bell on a tiger's neck":

   * Once upon a time a group of Buddhist monks gathered to answer one of their master's questions: Who can untie a bell hanging from the tiger's neck? Each had meditated at length on the issue and had come up with some conclusions and suggestions. One monk said: "Wait until the tiger is exhausted and asleep, then silently, slowly, and carefully untie it." Another said: "Feed the tiger until he is stuffed and content, then it wouldn't think about eating you. But practice beforehand to curb your fear as you approach." An old monk laughed at them and said, "You're playing with danger. None of your methods are really safe. A tiger is a tiger — always unpredictable around humans and always wild. The tiger must be bound with strong cords before the bell can be untied from around its neck." Another monk piped up and asked the older monk: "Who would tie the tiger up before trying to untie the bell?" The older monk hadn't considered that small detail, and they were all stumped.

    Finally they went back to Tai Qin, their master who had posed their question, to share their solutions with him. With each answer he laughed louder, which disconcerted them. Then he looked at them hard and said: "Who bound the tiger and tied the bell around its neck in the first place? Obviously that is the person who knows how to untie the bell hanging from the tiger's neck."

A parable answers questions by posing new ones and pointing out the gaps in our thinking, in our perceptions, and in our approach to life individually and collectively. Parables reveal by throwing curves, or by opening trap doors underneath the floor on which we're standing and saying: What if everything you're thinking … What if everything you're sure of ... What if you're on the wrong tack, the wrong track ... What if you're not anywhere near aware of what is actually happening.... What if you've been living your life this way because of what you get out of it rather than because it's actually a graceful way to live? What if? Because all the parables deal with crucial issues in everyone's life — money, pay, survival, the state of economics, dominance, violence, destructive power, nationalism, food, seeds, allegiance, relationships, authority, fear and subservience due to insecurity or collusion, especially with those who profit from evil, lying, robbery, pain and suffering. The parables elicit many reactions: frequently, an initial silence, confusion, then flickers of awareness, the realization of being confronted, challenged, accused, told the truth — followed by anger, conflicting emotions, being frozen and stuck in place, rationalization, panic, the need to run, stampede — then as grace works within — a tearful need for repentance, conversion, and obedience. The parable breaks into our minds and hearts and lives, shattering our complacency and upending our usual modes of being, with intensity and immediacy that demand that we respond NOW. And when we respond and act, another piece reveals itself, another area opens up, a new truth asserts itself, and the parable process is set in motion as layer upon layer of meaning, unfolds, and calls to change. There is no limit to the interpretations ... only the one placed on the parable by hearers who stop changing and stop understanding and refuse to listen. The parable shuts us out until we return with openness, with a need to hear.

So a parable elicits as many reactions to the telling, to the content, as there are people listening: laughter, confusion, annoyance, misunderstanding, disorientation, anger, rejection, resistance, rationalization, denial. You can't say that! You don't know anything about me! Outright refusal or silence might indicate the beginnings of reflection and the response Jesus hoped for when he told the stories: repentance, conversions, submission to the will of God, taking the truth to heart, confession of sin, and intention to repair the world, restore relationships, undo the harm we have done, and bring the kingdom of heaven more truly upon the earth. Often when I teach about the parables someone says: "No wonder they killed him, telling stories like that and going after people." Or, "I'm surprised that he lasted as long as he did." These parables can get you killed. It is one of the ways that Jesus resists being sucked into the ways of the institutions of religion, economics, politics, and nationalism. Through their content as well as through their method, they teach his followers who struggle in the same situations across time and place,

In chapter 13, Jesus relates a set of parables that use many images — seeds (especially mustard seed), sowers, weeds, wheat, yeast, buried treasure, pearls of great worth, a drag net thrown into the sea. And at the end of the tales, Jesus asks his disciples "Do you understand all these things?" And they say, "Yes!" Then Jesus describes who is truly a scribe in his kingdom — a follower who writes down teachings of the master for encouragement, for continued study and conversion of life, for the next generations and for growth in obedience and understanding of the wisdom of God. He says:

> Then every scribe who has been instructed in the kingdom
> of heaven is like the head of a household who brings from
> his storeroom both the new and the old. (Mt 13:52)

Jesus concludes his Parable of the Sower with the refrain: "Whoever has ears ought to hear." Sometimes this line is translated: "Those who have ears should listen" (NIRV). It is an exhortation. These are not nice little stories or allegorical descriptions; they are holes to fall into and know that you have fallen into the hands of the living God. He reminds us that we are privileged to hear these parables and must take them to heart. The chapter ends with his own rejecting him totally in Nazareth. This is his reason for telling parables — to speak the wisdom he knows with God the Father and yet not "throw ... pearls before swine," who don't know the difference between corn husks and items of great value. Telling parables is one way Jesus leads a lifestyle of resistance, and he will become more pointed with the stories as certain groups formulate their opposition against him more clearly by plotting to kill him. Jesus himself is the parable of God in living flesh and blood, bone and marrow, word and deed. Some will seek not only to kill the teller, hoping the story will no longer be heard, but to kill the dream, eliminating not only the words but the flesh and life of the Parable of God, Jesus, beloved child and obedient servant who is truer than any other Word ever spoken. We will look at a few of Jesus' parables now, and more in the next chapter where they are part of Jesus' resistance, even unto torture and death. Each time Jesus tells the stories and preaches, with each parable, he makes stronger and stronger demands, widening and deepening the gap between those who are listening and those who are refusing to be open to the Word.

Chapter 25 contains three parables. The first, that of the Ten Virgins, ends with the warning: " ... [H]e [the bridegroom] said ... 'Amen I say to you: I do not know you.' Therefore, stay awake, for you know neither the day nor the hour" (Mt 25:12–13). It foreshadows the judgment we all will face — whether Jesus will acknowledge us when the kingdom comes, now upon the earth and finally in the fullness of the wedding feast in heaven's glory. The second, The Parable of the Talents, appears both in Luke and in Matthew. The chapter concludes with the Parable of the Sheep and the Goats, also referred to as the Parable of the Judgment of the Nations. After telling these three, Jesus goes into Jerusalem to die. These parables must be read in the shadow of intrigue, hatred, massing of his enemies, and the coming feast of the Passover. Let's consider the Parable of the Talents first:

> Therefore, stay awake, for you know neither the day nor the hour. It will be as when a man who was going on a journey called in his servants and entrusted his possessions to them. To one he gave five talents; to another, two; to a third, one — to each according to his ability. Then he went away. Immediately the one who received five talents went and traded with them, and made another five. Likewise, the one who received two made another two. But the man who received one went off and dug a hole in the ground and buried his master's money. (Mt 25:13–18)

Like most, this parable is based on ordinary occurrences of every-day life. A man, obviously very wealthy, goes on a journey of some length, and entrusts his possessions to three servants. (Events in these kinds of stories often come in threes, and the third is the one that reveals wisdom.) As would happen in real life, he does not distribute his money equally. The one who gets more makes more as does the one who gets some. But the one who gets the least buries it, and is thus able to return no more than what he received. Jesus' listeners would be hooked, curious to see how things go. Reckoning time comes when the master returns.

> * After a long time the master of those servants came back and settled accounts with them. The one who had received five talents came forward bringing the additional five. He said, "Master, you gave me five talents. See, I have made five more." His master said to him, "Well done, my good and faithful servant. Since you were faithful in small matters, I will give you great responsibilities. Come, share your master's joy." (Then) the one who had received two talents also came forward and said, "Master, you gave me two talents. See, I have made two more." His master said to him, "Well done, my good and faithful servant. Since you were faithful in small matters, I will give you great responsibilities. Come, share your master's joy." Then the one who had received the one talent came forward and said: "Master, I knew you were a demanding person, harvesting where you did not plant and gathering where you did not scatter, so out of fear I went off and buried your talent in the ground. Here it is back." His master said to him in reply, "You wicked, lazy servant! So you knew that I harvest where I did not plant and gather where I did not scatter? Should you not then have put my money in the bank so that I could have gotten it back with interest on my return? Now then! Take the talent from him and give it to the one with ten." (Mt 25:19–28)

So far, nothing unusual has happened. This is the way of the world and the way those who collude with the state, the wealthy who control economies and even religious bodies, accommodate themselves to dominant power structures. Those listening to the story know how life operates and in their master's opinion the first two made it up on the world's ladder of success. The audience, however, would have been waiting to see what's going to happen to the third servant. They would have empathized with the man described as fearful in the face of those who control life, death, slavery, debtors' prison, property, and so forth. If they'd thought of it, they too might have put the master's money in the bank, although many might have just buried it in the ground as the fearful servant did. And there is nothing unusual in the description of the master: he is shrewd, dishonest, excellent at making a profit, demanding and in a sense ruthless when it comes to his money — those who imitate him get to share in it, but those who don't face stiff consequences.

There are two ways in which this parable has been misinterpreted. The first is construing the word "talent" to mean personal attributes and gifts rather than enormous amounts of money, thereby blunting the edge of its judgment of economics and collusion between groups that have power. The parable is not about the psychology of the individual, but about moral choices in society that must be faced at judgment time. The second, more problematic misinterpretation sees the master as God at Judgment Day. Such a God doesn't look or act anything like the Father Jesus describes and prays to, our Father, just and merciful beyond measure, who acts truthfully in regard to all and whose power has nothing to do with the powers of the world. Our Father is hardly "a demanding person, harvesting where he did not plant and gathering where he did not scatter," striking such fear in those given responsibility in the kingdom of heaven on earth that their only response is paralysis and burying it away. In other of Jesus' stories such as the Parable of the Sower (Mt 13:3–9), the thing put into the ground yields massive, outrageous returns: "Some seed fell on rich soil, and produced fruit, a hundred or sixty or thirtyfold" (Mt 13:8). Such seed produces a harvest that will feed people, not the mere piling up of money and interest that benefits only those who already have more. Even the yeast buried in three measures of wheat flour will feed great numbers of people when it expands.

When Jesus does speak of finding buried treasure, he suggests the opposite: instead of putting valuables in banks for interest or trading on the market for profit, we're supposed to rebury the treasure, rejoice exceedingly, and then go sell everything we have to buy the field. That is exactly what those who heard the Word of God and took it to heart did, and together they became the harvest, the food for others. And when we buy the field, we get the treasure too! Let's look at the ending of this parable of the talents:

> Now then! Take the talent from him and give it to the one with ten. For to everyone who has, more will be given and he will grow rich; but from the one who has not, even what he has will be taken away. And throw this useless servant into the darkness outside, where there will be wailing and grinding of teeth. (Mt 25:28–30)

In the parable with which chapter 25 begins, Jesus tells a parable about the preparations for a wedding feast. Through it, he wants to let the community know whom he will recognize as belonging to him in the kingdom at judgment time. It deals with the wise, who have kept oil in their lamps, and the foolish, who have let the oil run out (the oil representing the Spirit, as well as the waters of baptism). At the bridegroom's coming, those who are prepared don't share their oil with those who have none. There are some things that each person must gain for him or herself, making a choice for conversion and selling all they have for what is needed — oil in their lamps, or pearls of great worth, or treasures in fields. Those who run off to buy what they lack get caught outside the locked doors and when they plead to come in are told firmly: " 'Amen, I say to you, I do not know you.' Therefore, stay awake," Jesus says, "for you know neither the day nor the hour" (Mt 25 12–13). This will be the justice of God, who will welcome those who were faithful but will exclude those who during their lives were inattentive, unfaithful, or unmindful that the kingdom of justice and peace was coming. In the second parable, that of the talents, Jesus looks at the world of economic, national, and social power. He tells what happens in the world when judgment comes.

Those who have get more. Those with little, however, or those who refuse to play the game, lose what they have however, and are cast out of the presence of the powerful, who remain intent on increasing their profit and extending their holdings and who rejoice with those who, like them, have also learned to turn a profit with the resources they have been given. Jesus follows this pronouncement by describing how, after gathering and separating out all the nations of the world, the Son of Man will render judgment. He will use his own criteria, which are very different from anything found in structures controlled by those given to Satan. Each of us must choose whether to accept the kingdom of heaven coming upon the earth and remain faithful to that choice day in and day out in the society where we live, notwithstanding that society's greed, violence, competition, and inequality. Jesus tells us that at the end, judgment will be based on God's Word in Jesus, not on the values that operate in our economies and nations. These are words Jesus says at the end of the parable of the weeds and wheat in chapter 13:

> The Son of Man will send his angels, and they will collect out of his kingdom all who cause others to sin and all evil-doers. They will throw them into the fiery furnace, where there will be wailing and grinding of teeth. Then the righteous will shine like the sun in the kingdom of their Father. Whoever has ears ought to hear. (Mt 13:41–43)

And in the same chapter, following the parable about the treasure buried in the field and the net thrown into the sea, he says this:

> Thus it will be at the end of the age. The angels will go out and separate the wicked from the righteous and throw them into the fiery furnace, where there will be wailing and grinding of teeth. Do you understand all these things? (Mt 13:49–51)

Many in Matthew's church knew what happened to those who tried to operate within the political, social, and economic structures imposed by the Roman Empire, even to those Jewish leaders who had accommodated Roman practices in an attempt to survive under occupation. The Temple was destroyed, and there was fire and gnashing of teeth. They had lost it all. And Matthew's community of Christians, Jews, and Gentiles found itself in the precarious place of that last servant who had tried to escape his master's harsh judgment by burying his talent in the ground. Trapped within the Empire and consigned to the fringes of the Jewish nation, they were ostracized, persecuted, and martyred. Many had to decide whether to follow in Jesus' footsteps and literally walk all the way to the cross and death and resurrection, or against Jesus' exhortation, to attempt serving two masters and still have the kingdom of heaven on earth and in heaven too. Jesus finishes with the parable of judgment according to the Son of Man, God's foreman from the vineyard. This, Jesus' last story, is the most powerful of the parables, especially when viewed in light of his being thrown outside the city, hung on a tree, reviled and scorned and destroyed by those who serve masters other than God the Father. Most of us have heard these words before and think we've grasped what they say, but listen again to the details:

> When the Son of Man comes in his glory, and all the angels with him, he will sit upon his glorious throne, and all the nations will be assembled before him. And he will separate them one from another, as a shepherd separates the sheep from the goats. He will place the sheep on his right and the goats on his left. (Mt 25:31–34)

The scene opens with the Son of Man, the one who has taught all nations and who will judge them, on a throne, a seat of judgment as well as mercy. In this court scene there are no defense lawyers; all nations and all peoples are judged according to the same criteria. Unlike the parable of the talents, judgment is rendered in a very different way. First, the Judge is called the Son of Man. In the next chapter we will look at this appellation more carefully, for this is Jesus as he sees himself, his own identity, the source of his actions. As Son of Man he has many human characteristics, but the wisdom of the Son of God. He judges from a position of power that includes both heaven and earth. He will render universal justice, not only upon individuals but upon nations and upon groups who dwell in those nations. Recalling Psalm 23, in the tradition of Moses and David, he is described as a shepherd. A shepherd is concerned with unity, with community, with keeping together all his sheep, whom he knows intimately and who listen to his voice. He provides forage,

water, nurture, protection, safety and security as well as companionship; he saves the lost, the hurt, the strays. As we saw in chapter 5, a
shepherd will go to great lengths in order to save even one of his
sheep — leaving ninety-nine alone in the field so that the weakest
might be brought back home. This shepherd-judge begins by separating all nations into two distinct flocks — goats and sheep.

One group of nations is described as "goats." Goats eat anything
and everything. Goats are fiercely independent. They group together
loosely and go their own ways, climbing and scattering for forage.
Within days they can strip the vegetation from a terrain, eating the bark
off trees, lichen, and anything else they find. They are temperamental
and belligerent, butting heads and fighting over food, turf, and relationships. When slaughtered they scream, even after their throats have
been cut. This is one group of nations.

The other is described as "sheep." For the most part, sheep graze
placidly. They are often described as docile and stupid, but they recognize the voice of the one they belong to; only a very sick sheep will
follow a voice other than the one of its shepherd. They need to be led,
pastured, and cared for, and are easily frightened and skittish, stam-
peding without much provocation. When they do panic, they trample
their own young. They often have trouble recognizing their own after
the lambs have been shorn, yet orphaned lambs will bond with another
ewe if a piece of wool from its dead mother is wrapped around the
surrogate mother. When slaughtered, they submit meekly and silently
— hence the description of Jesus as the Lamb of God, although unlike
a passive sheep he consciously refused to be violent in the face of death
and died forgiving those who brutalized and murdered him. This is the
other group of nations.

At judgment time the decree is announced:

> Then the king will say to those on his right. "Come,
> you who are blessed by my Father. Inherit the kingdom
> prepared for you from the foundation of the world. For I
> was hungry and you gave me food, I was thirsty and you
> gave me drink, a stranger and you welcomed me, naked and
> you clothed me, ill and you cared for me, in prison and you

visited me." Then the righteous will answer him and say, "Lord, when did we see you hungry and feed you, or thirsty and give you drink? When did we see you a stranger and welcome you, or naked and clothe you? When did we see you ill or in prison and visit you?" And the king will say to them in reply, "Amen, I say to you, whatever you did for one of these least brothers of mine, you did for me." (Mt 25:34–40)

The first group, the "sheep" are drawn into the kingdom on earth and its fullness in heaven. They seem surprised that they have met the demands and fit the descriptions of what they have done! The criteria are the corporal works of mercy, giving every human being what is rightly and justly due by nature of their being human. Jesus' theological explanation has profound consequences — the hungry, the thirsty, the stranger, the naked, the prisoner are the Incarnation. Because God has assumed human flesh and blood in Jesus, now, as the children of God, reconciled to our Father, whatever we do, especially to the least of our brothers and sisters, we do to God, who takes it personally that in doing it for one another we have done it for him. This is the essence of worship and life, ethics and spirituality. We are saved by bringing his kingdom to earth, which means in essence to provide food, water, clothing, and protection from the elements; to heal the sick, to draw in and protect the stranger and the outsider; to align ourselves with and to visit the imprisoned. This is how Matthew's own church experienced society and it is to be our own place and work, service and worship in our society today.

Then justice is rendered a second time. The same criteria are laid out to the "goats" and they respond with the same question as did the sheep: "Lord, when did we see you hungry or thirsty or a stranger or naked or ill or in prison, and not minister to your needs?" And the Son of Man responds the same way: " 'Amen, I say to you, what you did not do for one of these least ones, you did not do for me.' And those will go off to eternal punishment, but the righteous to eternal life" (Mt 25:45–46). When we have had the opportunity, whatever we refuse or choose to ignore or to not do in regard to the least ones, we refuse or choose to ignore or not do for God. This is what Jesus has been doing and what he has been teaching from the beginning. It is up to us to act like the beloved children of God, not like those out for themselves who think they can honor or worship God the Father, Jesus' God in the obedience of the Spirit's power, while at the same time ignoring the glimpses of the kingdom of heaven in the parables and in Jesus himself, who is the Parable of God in flesh and blood, heart, mind, and soul among us.

Note that in this parable of the Last Judgment, the Son of Man directs his judgment toward groups. Certainly, each of us must answer for how we have lived out the corporal works of mercy; but Jesus makes it clear that we also must answer for how our nations, our churches, our dioceses, our religious communities, our families have lived them out too. This is a sobering, challenging, demanding call to conversion — as are all of Jesus' parables, especially these last three before he will stand before the nations of his world and find that he will be destroyed for the truth he tells and the Truth he is.

* Let me conclude with a story that echoes Jesus' own parables. It actually happened, and continues to happen every week at the Wailing Wall, the last remaining remnant of the Temple in Jerusalem. At the beginning of every Sabbath a group of women who call themselves "The Women in Black" gather there to pray. Dressed in black chadors, the women chant Kaddish, the Jewish prayer of mourning for the dead. Facing the wall, they sing first for all the people of Israel who have died that week in the fighting; then with their backs to the wall, for all the people of Palestine who have died. They have been doing this for years and they elicit a wide range of reactions — from violent insults to compassionate solidarity.

One Sabbath, they turned from the wall only to face a hostile group of rabbinical seminarians and their teachers who spit on them while shouting curses. One man in particular spit repeatedly in the face the woman who was leading the prayers as she tried to pray. The encounter grew more heated, threatening to escalate into physical violence. The leader, a diminu-

tive woman, stopped her prayer to speak with the man trying
to provoke her with such strong insults: "I know exactly how
you feel. I have felt the same way too, with my heart filled with
hatred and wanting to kill." Those shouting insults fell silent.
In a tear-choked voice she continued, "Six years ago in a
suicide bombing I lost my beloved daughter, my fourteen year
old daughter, and I wanted to kill. I wanted to kill anyone, to
make someone suffer for my loss, anyone, I didn't care who,
and for months I lived like that. And then I slowly began to
realize that I had become just like the people I blamed and
hated. I was becoming inhuman and incapable of love, of
kindness or simple courtesies. I despised myself. And that's
when I realized there are only two kinds of people in the world.
There are those whose response to everything that happens is
rage, hate, violence and disruption, getting even and taking it
out on someone else. And there are those whose response to
everything that happens is love, forgiveness, to seek understanding, reconciliation, peace-making and realizing we are
all the same — we ache and bleed the same way; we wail and
grieve the same way; we love the same things — life, our families, our God, our country, our grandchildren. And I had to
decide which group I belonged to: those who hate and kill or
those who love and make peace."

Her voice dropped. "I decided. Now it is time for you to
decide — which group will you belong to? Which kind of
power will you serve and obey? Will you be filled with hate or
love, revenge or making peace? You decide now." Heavy,
hard silence followed. Then the man spit at her full in the face,
cursed her, turned, and walked away. She nearly buckled but
she pulled herself together, stood with the other women in
black, and began with a cracked voice that grew surer and
clearer with each word she prayed. And then it happened —
the students and teachers separated themselves. Some spit on
the ground and walked away, but others stood shoulder to
shoulder with the women, not touching them, but praying
Kaddish together.

This story affords us a glimpse of the vision of judgment. That encounter at the Wailing Wall was an incident of the kingdom of the prophets coming upon the earth. It was hope and light and power to be embraced. Right there and then they had to decide — just as we must do every time we hear one of Jesus' parables.

Questions

1. Which parable in this chapter bothers you the most? Why? What would you have to do to make the parable a reality in your life, with your family, community, and parish? What feeling rises up in you when you hear this Word of Jesus?

2. Which of the three people who are given talents most resembles you? Why? What have you done with yours? In your life, economically, socially, politically, nationally, or in a religious group, with whom are you in collusion? Do you try to work both sides of power rather than committing yourself to a group that holds you accountable to grow in faithfulness?

3. According to the criteria of the Last Judgment, if you were to be judged as a member of your nation, diocese, religious community, parish, or family, or as an individual, in which of the two groups would you find yourself? What does that make you feel? What is your reaction? Do you need to change groups?

4. What corporal work of mercy have you never practiced? Why? Choose one and start to do it on a weekly basis with a group so that you can talk about what it does to you each time. Have you ever thought that you could make it into the kingdom at judgment time by being associated with a particular group? Do you belong to a group of peacemakers, those who work for the preservation of human life from conception to natural death, prison reform, universal health care, shelter, clean water, food distribution, or the daily needs of those lacking the basic necessities? If not, perhaps it's time.

9

Resistance, unto
Death on the Cross

Jesus walks the way of his Father, a way that will culminate in the cross and a death that leads to resurrection and life that will not die. From the very beginning of his mission on earth, even as a newborn, Jesus faced opposition. The very thought that the baby Jesus might be the presence of justice and peace, of light and truth that would lead all peoples and nations to the knowledge that God was with his people — as Emmanuel — led King Herod to seek his life. From the beginning of his ministry, as he becomes aware of God as his beloved Father, and our Father, all of us the beloved children of God, in the power of the Spirit, Jesus struggles as he becomes aware that many would take exception to those he embraced, and would oppose all that he said, all that he did, even his very presence in the world. Jesus resists inside himself through prayer and reliance on his Father and the Spirit; he resists outside himself through his preaching and his actions, particularly by calling his disciples to follow him and imitate him. He resists empire and nation, economics and politics, society and traditions, institutions and individuals, community leaders. His unassailable integrity, truthfulness, and embrace of the scorned and despised, even sinners and nonbelievers, leads him to the ultimate resistance: giving his complete self — body, life, and heart — to who will kill him, resistance unto death.

Jesus, the Word of God made flesh, the Parable of God, the Presence of God, the kingdom of heaven on earth, Emmanuel must resist most strongly the leaders of institutional religion and the leaders of the empire that occupy the land where he lives, a resistance no less crucial — and deadly — today for those who believe in Jesus and seek to follow him. The forces that oppose Jesus come together when he has finished preaching to all who are open to his Word of truth and when he is living among sinners. Matthew states what will happen, how it will happen, and why:

> When Jesus had finished all these words, he said to his disciples. "You know that in two days' time it will be Passover, and the Son of Man will be handed over to be crucified." Then the chief priests and the elders of the people assembled in the palace of the high priest, who was called Caiaphas, and they consulted together to arrest Jesus by treachery and put him to death. But they said, "Not during the festival, that there may not be a riot among the people." (Mt 26:1–5)

Matthew makes Jesus' awareness of his impending arrest and execution and the elders' decision seem clear-cut, but these events occurred in a swirl of confusion. During his entire public ministry, Jesus had been speaking the truth about the Jewish elders, lawyers, scribes, and teachers and about their collusion in the human misery that the Roman occupation brought upon their nation. But Matthew is writing nearly fifty years after the death of Jesus. He is writing after the destruction of the Temple in Jerusalem, Nero's execution of many first generation leaders in the church, the expulsion of fledgling Christian communities from synagogues and from the practice of Jewish life and religion, and during persecutions by the Romans that rose and fell in intensity, duration and place. His frightened communities needed to be encouraged and reminded that like Jesus they too might have to pay the price for speaking truthfully about who they were as Followers of the Way and believers in Jesus. Because they belonged to a community that stood out for having "no poor among them" (Acts and, later, the Didache), they could not avoid being asked, "Are you one of them?"

Very early on in Matthew's Gospel, therefore, even as Jesus sends his disciples out to preach, in his name, the good news of the kingdom of heaven come among the children of earth, he tells the disciples about the coming persecutions. The first detailed and horrible mention of persecution is based on what Matthew's communities had been experiencing seventy or eighty years after Jesus' death:

> Behold, I am sending you like sheep in the midst of wolves; so be shrewd as serpents and simple as doves. But beware of people, for they will hand you over to courts and scourge you in their synagogues, and you will be led before governors and kings for my sake as a witness before them and the pagans. When they hand you over, do not worry about how you are to speak or what you are to say. You will be given at the moment what you are to say. For it will not be you who speak but the Spirit of your Father speaking through you. Brother will hand over brother to death, and the father his child; children will rise up against parents and have them put to death. You will be hated by all because of my name, but whoever endures to the end will be saved. When they persecute you in one town, flee to another. (Mt 10:16–23)

The brutal persecutions invaded and tore apart every human relationship — family and community. Choosing to be the brother or sister of Jesus may very well come at the price of family ties and social position. He tries to tell his disciples to hang on to a dearer and truer life while being faithful in this one, which they treasure so dearly, and rightly so. But Jesus' realistic words remind them not to be naïve about anyone, even members of their own families, churches, and communities. Matthew is describing what they have been experiencing during the past seven or eight decades. Yet he is also reminding them of the power and presence of the Spirit of the Father, the Spirit of Jesus also active and expressive in their lives. They have been given words of wisdom that come singing and shining through them, confounding their persecutors and witnessing in such a way that others came to believe in them as they preserved their faith and persevered as Jesus' brothers and sisters.

Jesus' words remind them that he is peace itself, the peace God the Father has shared with all peoples, a peace diametrically opposed to the powers of the world, a peace that those who refuse the Good News cannot recognize. These words of Jesus describe what they have suffered because of their choice to belong first to the family of God:

> Do not think that I have come to bring peace upon the earth. I have come to bring not peace but the sword. For I have come to set a man "against his father, a daughter against her mother, and a daughter-in-law against her mother-in-law; and one's enemies will be those of his household." (Mt 10:34–36)

Such a sobering and frightful version of peace cannot be ignored — Jesus describes the double-edged sword of the Word of God that pierces every heart and separates those who believe from those who do not. In addition, Jesus reminds them that "No disciple is above his teacher, no slave above his master. It is enough for the disciple that he become like his teacher, for the slave that he become like his master.... If they have called the master of the house Beelzebul, how much more those of his household!" (Mt 10:24–25). In his steadfastness, Jesus endured opposition and rejection, name-calling, being cursed, and eventually humiliation, torture, crucifixion, and death. If we remain faithful, we should not be surprised if we receive some of the same reactions. These are descriptions of the last group of those blessed: those persecuted for the sake of righteousness. Along with the poor, those who know such persecution are already in the grace and freedom of the kingdom of heaven, in the power of the Spirit and the Word and intimacy with the Father, that Jesus himself knew and as he was known. In chapter 10 Jesus begins with the clear call to the cross and he will build on it, extending it beyond physical crucifixion to a way of life, a spirituality of mind and awareness of heart that consciously keeps choosing to walk the way with Jesus, the master, the teacher, and the beloved of God:

> Whoever loves father or mother more than me is not worthy of me, and whoever loves son or daughter more than me is not

worthy of me; and whoever does not take up his cross and
follow after me is not worthy of me. Whoever finds his life
will lose it, and whoever loses his life for my sake will find it.

Whoever receives you receives me, and whoever receives
me receives the one who sent me. Whoever receives a
prophet because he is a prophet will receive a prophet's
reward and whoever receives a righteous man because he
is righteous will receive a righteous man's reward. And
whoever gives only a cup of cold water to one of these little
ones to drink because he is a disciple — amen, I say to you, he
will surely not lose his reward. (Mt 10:37–42)

This passage describes Matthew's own church and communities.
They are experiencing persecution and martyrdom, including loss
of property, family connections, place in the synagogue or in Jewish
society. They are the ones left behind to practice the works of mercy,
to care for the least in the community — believers and unbelievers
alike — because they are the children of their Father, the brothers
and sisters of Jesus. Each will receive his or her reward. God knows
and sees each of them. Each is a part of the community as prophet, or
one of those who do justice, those who form the communities of the
Beatitudes, those who by resisting lose what is precious to them
(selling all they have for the treasure and the pearl) and those called
to stand up for following Jesus and who know the cross because of
what they say and do before empire and synagogue.

Jesus calls us to follow him as the Son of Man, even to the cross.
But what does it mean for believers to face the cross? Especially,
what did it mean for Matthew's church? Most of us resist the
cross. We ignore those pieces of the gospel which demand that
we take a stand, that we must decide, that we cannot have both
God and money. We let the dominant cultures, races, economies,
political parties and nations compromise our lives, limiting religion
to certain small areas of personal influence such as sexuality, family
relationships, or purely individual acts. We avoid holding ourselves
accountable for our major choices, for the associations we form, for
our public actions. This is reason that Jesus refers to the disruption

of family relationships as a consequence of facing the cross. Living the gospel truly will alienate others and antagonize family. If we have not experienced such alienation and antagonism, perhaps we must examine our lives with the eye of the Spirit of God to see whether we have stopped our ears and blinded ourselves to the heart of the Word of God — the cross. Perhaps we can get a better sense of what it means to follow the Son of Man, even to the cross, through the story of a master craftsman and his apprentice:

* Once upon a time a master violin maker wanted to choose a disciple to take his place. He had painstakingly shown each of his students every aspect of making a violin, from choosing the wood and aging it for many years, to hand-carving and shaping the pieces, to the final varnishing. One young woman was superb in nearly every aspect of the craft. The only skill she lacked, though, was probably the most important — she couldn't seem to be able to determine which tree held the best wood for a violin.

Again and again he had taken her out to look at the trees. He took her during the spring thaws and strong winds, the hot summers, and especially at the shift of seasons from autumn when the leaves dropped to the harshness of winter. And they had hard winters: brutal cold with long periods when ice collected on the trees, breaking limbs; furious winds and blowing snow. Standing in the barren forests he would ask her, "Which trees hold the wood of the violin?" Invariably she would pick ones that didn't look like they were taking a beating, trees protected by others from the worst of the weather; or she would chose trees for their graceful appearance even during the storms. But he knew that the wood of the trees she chose would not produce violins of superb quality. She had surely learned all the other skills, but he began to despair of teaching her how to make this first and most crucial choice. So he took her out to the same forest one more time and in a gale they stood facing the trees. And he asked her to talk about the trees. She felt sorry for the battered ones, those taking the initial force, ones that formed a weatherbreak for the trees behind. As she spoke of her sorrow at how they cracked and bent and even split in the blizzard, he realized why she was making her choices. "Look at them," he commanded. "Listen to the limbs in the wind. Close your eyes and know they are the ones being 'tuned'!" In that moment she knew and understood and opened her eyes to see those standing in the forefront, those that stood and faced the elements were already "making music," having absorbed all of stresses of the elements. From their wood she could make instruments capable of magnificent sound.

What the storm was doing to the trees is what Jesus is trying to do with his disciples, and with all of us. The weathering, the stripping, even the harshness of outside forces are part of the process to make us disciples, truthful and alive with the music of the kingdom of heaven within us. Living the Way, picking up and bearing our cross, the works of mercy and forgiveness are tuning us for the music of handing over our lives daily, sometimes completely, to service of the kingdom of justice and peace and love.

More than any other gospel, Matthew's is suffused with negative forces — conflict, aggression, demonizing others by name-calling and judging them as not human, and religious authority devoid of compassion. The disputes between Jesus and the leaders reflect the very real conflict in Matthew's communities between the small churches and synagogues, as they attempted to live together with their newly initiated Gentile converts in Jewish neighborhoods and quarters. Both groups live by the Torah and the traditions, but these new churches have come to believe that Jesus, who is greater than any prophet of the past, is the one who interprets the law most truthfully.

The community struggled with internal conflict and dissension between Jews and Gentiles and, depending on how the laws were interpreted, among those whom they welcomed, served with compassion, invited to the table. They forgave and reconciled reluctantly (reflected in Peter's question of precisely how many times he must forgive) and they struggled over who would lead them, and how: whether to copy the familiar synagogue and temple structure or whether to be as children, servants of all and the least in the community. Arguments erupted over legislation and the need to stop judging others and to acknowledge their own sometimes glaring faults. They succumbed to anger.

Jesus begins his Sermon on the Mount with images of anger and murder to emphasize what lies at the base of interpreting and practicing the law so that it gives life and does not demean and destroy others, extending it even to loving one's enemies. And they are to love not in isolation but with others, in a community of accountability.

Some within Matthew's community, even the leaders and teachers of the synagogue, sow dissension and continue to be harsh with others, rather than remembering that in Jesus' family, mercy rules and has the last word — always.

Jesus warns them repeatedly of the old leaven that can sour everything. Any teaching that dehumanizes others and does not bring forth abundant life must be shunned; leadership among his own followers cannot deteriorate into self-aggrandizement, self-absorption, and self-righteousness. And immediately after warning them to "beware [not] of the leaven of bread, but of the teaching of the Pharisees and Sadducees" (Mt 16:12), Jesus speaks forthrightly for the first time of the cross, passion, and death that he must embrace, as must his disciples and the leaders within the community:

> From that time on, Jesus began to show his disciples that he must go to Jerusalem and suffer greatly from the elders, the chief priests and the scribes, and be killed and on the third day be raised. (Mt 16:21)

Just after this announcement, Peter refuses to listen and attempts to sideline Jesus by pointing out the error of his ways. Jesus reacts strongly, calling Peter "Satan," the hinderer, making him confront the reality that even after his confession of faith and being entrusted with the keys of forgiveness, reconciliation, and atonement on behalf of the community, he is still thinking the way everyone else thinks. And Jesus' second statement about what would happen to the Son of Man, that he " … is to be handed over to men, and they will kill him, and he will be raised on the third day" (Mt 17:22–23), causes the disciples great grief.

The last time Jesus asks them to consider what is happening, he provides a more detailed explanation of what he will have to endure when handed over to the Jewish leadership, who in turn will hand him over to the Gentiles, the Romans, who will scourge, mock, and crucify him. But his disciples ignore him, and Matthew makes no mention of the effect these words have on them. Jesus has asked for their companionship three times and each time has been rebuffed. In fact, the third time he pleads with them to stay with him during his sufferings and death, James and John have their mother go to Jesus to ask that he give them the privileged places of honor and power on his right and left when he comes into power. She does not really understand what she is asking for on their behalf, and it causes anger among the disciples. Jesus draws them together and tells them clearly how to use the power that he shares with them:

> But Jesus summoned them and said, "You know that the rulers of the Gentiles lord it over them, and the great ones make their authority felt. But it shall not be so among you. Rather, whoever wishes to be great among you shall be your servant; whoever wishes to be first among you shall be your slave. Just so, the Son of Man did not come to be served but to serve and to give his life as a ransom for many." (Mt 20:25–28)

Jesus castigates the Roman leaders and anyone who acts as they do. Those who wish intimacy with Jesus, to share in his power, must become servants, even slaves. They are to resemble the Son of Man who has come to serve and to hand over his life to ransom the lives of others — a far cry from how authority and power has been and sometimes still is exercised in religious institutions, even within the church. Jesus issues this last injunction and reminder of the brutality that awaits him and those who truly practice what he preaches as he enters Jerusalem for his last week, to celebrate the Passover and to die.

At the height of hostilities between Jesus and the Pharisees,[1] Jesus confronts some of them about their collusion with the Roman empire. They try to set Jesus up to reveal whether he acknowledges the right of the empire to demand taxes from those they enslave:

> Then the Pharisees went off and plotted how they might entrap him in speech. They sent their disciples to him, with the Herodians, saying, "Teacher, we know that you are a truthful man and that you teach the way of God in accordance with the truth. And you are not concerned with anyone's opinion, for you do not regard a person's status. Tell us, then, what is your opinion: Is it lawful to pay the census tax to Caesar or not?" (Mt 22:15–17)

The disciples of the Herodians and the Pharisees detested each other, but they see a common enemy in Jesus. With oily praise they actually speak the truth, but with the intent to kill. They know who Jesus is: a teacher of the way of God who speaks the truth without subterfuge or the need to court others' opinion. In fact, they describe Jesus' forthrightness by contrasting it with those who live on the opinion of certain others and always take into consideration the status and wealth of the person with whom they are in dialogue — a description of themselves. But Jesus knows them all too well:

> Knowing their malice, Jesus said, "Why are you testing me, you hypocrites? Show me the coin that pays the census tax." Then they handed him the Roman coin. He said to them, "Whose image is this and whose inscription?" They replied, "Caesar's." At that he said to them, "Then repay to Caesar what belongs to Caesar and to God what belongs to God." When they heard this they were amazed, and leaving him they went away. (Mt 22: 18–22)

---

1. Many exegetes now believe that Jesus himself may have been a Pharisee because of the way they stay at him and the way he continues to speak to them with a familiarity that would denote inclusion in the group. In a sense he does not give up on them and tries to use all his resources and wisdom to win them over.

This encounter takes place in the outer courtyard of the Temple, where Jesus is teaching. There were strict laws about the money used in Temple transactions. Roman coins had to be exchanged for Temple currency to buy anything carried into the temple area or to purchase animals for sacrifice. These Pharisees should not even have been holding the Roman coin that they produced. Moreover, the census tax to be paid with it was especially humiliating to the Jewish people who dwelled as slaves, counted as animals and beasts of burden in their own land. The coin itself, which contained an image of the head of Caesar and the inscription: "Augustus ... Divi Aug(usti) F(ilius)" ["Augustus ... son of the Divine Augustus"], reveals blasphemy by considering a human being, Augustus, to be a god. It violates the first two commandments of the covenant: Thou shalt not have any other god, and Thou shalt not have graven images. But why worry about blasphemy if it is part of a gambit to trap a despised enemy?

Rabbi Arthur Waskow has examined this scene carefully. Both Jesus and the teachers of both groups would have been familiar with the arguments concerning the issues of paying the tax and how the Jewish community and its leadership were to relate to those who held them in bondage. They had been topics of fierce debate for decades. First, Jesus traps them by asking them for the coin — they carry it with them, and so disobey Jewish law. Then, when he asks them whose image and inscription are on the coin they affirm together: "Caesar's!" But Jesus asks them clearly: "Whose image is this?" Certainly he is referring to the coin they hold in their hands; but, as the rabbi says, it may well have been that Jesus put his hand over the shoulder of the man holding the coin as he looked at him and said, "And whose image is this?", that is to say, " Whose image are you?" Rabbi Waskow continues his explanation of the episode in this way:

In the first chapter (Genesis) the Torah teaches that God made Adam — the human race — *b'tzelem elohim*, "in the image of God." What does this mean?

Our rabbis taught: Adam, the first human being, was created as a single person to show forth the greatness of the Ruler Who is Beyond all Rulers, the Blessed Holy One. For if a human ruler [like Caesar, the

Roman Emperor who was indeed the ruler in their time and place] mints many coins from one mold, they all carry the same image, they all look the same. But the Blessed Holy One shaped all human beings in the Divine Image, as Adam was shaped in the Divine Image (Gen 1:27) *"b'tzelem elohim"*, "in the Image of God." And yet not one of them resembles another.[2]

Let us absorb this. The rabbis drew an analogy between the image a human ruler — Caesar — puts upon the coins of the realm, and the Image the Infinite Ruler puts upon the many "coins" of humankind. The very diversity of human faces shows forth the Unity and Infinity of God, whereas the uniformity of imperial coins makes clear the limitations on the power of the emperor.[3]

The image on any coin is dead, the same representation over and over, with no individuality and no human worth, just empty, lifeless repetition. But Genesis tells us that we are made in the image and likeness of God and in that image there is multiplicity, diversity, singularity, uniqueness; we must never forget in whose image we are made and live. Realizing that in itself would have shocked and stunned the questioners. But Jesus goes on and gives a command, "Then repay to Caesar what belongs to Caesar and to God what belongs to God" (Mt 22:21). Rabbi Waskow restates what Jesus meant to say in this fashion:

* "Give your whole self to the One Who has imprinted Divinity upon you! — You, you who are one of the Rabbis, my brother Rabbi — you know that is the point of the story! All I have done is to remind you!"

The coin of the realm will matter very little, if the trouble-maker listens.

---

2. Soncino translated, p. 240 and quoted in Arthur Waskow from shalomctr@aol.com, October 6, 2004.

3. http://www.shalomctr.org/node/691.

So the questioner walks away, suddenly profoundly troubled by the life-question that he faces.[4]

All that we are and all that we have is to be at the service of God, and so shared with the needy in the community. And for Jesus' followers, all that is to be at the service even of one's needy enemies. We must never forget that we too are servants and slaves, summoned to give our lives as ransom for those who do not know the fullness of life. We should have nothing left over for the kingdoms of the earth and the powers that occupy, pillage, enslave, and murder. Our lives must provide a signal of hope, an alternative for those whose lives are burdened and meaningless under the heel of their oppressors. Jesus' answer and his total devotion to God leaves them speechless, and they walk away.

Jesus confronts every faction within the Jewish community, each with its own agenda, and he "bests" them all, using their own arguments and traditions, always returning to the necessity of mercy toward others, personal integrity that serves the community, and the necessity of faithfulness that transcends any law. In chapter 23 Jesus accuses them of insincerity, hypocrisy, hard-heartedness, brutality in demanding others live up to the letter of the law while doing nothing to ease their burdens, and judging others harshly while they themselves manipulate the law, deciding which to practice and which to conveniently ignore. In this chapter Matthew gathers into one discourse several of Jesus' statements that begin "Woe to you ... ," statements directed primarily at those who have responsibility for others and whose authority and teaching are meant to serve as models for imitation. He begins by speaking to the people directly:

> Then Jesus spoke to the crowds and to his disciples, saying,
> "The scribes and the Pharisees have taken their seat on the
> chair of Moses. Therefore, do and observe all things what-

---

4. From "God & Caesar: The Image on the Coin," http://www.shalomctr.org /node/691.

soever they tell you, but do not follow their example. For they preach but they do not practice. They tie up heavy burdens (hard to carry) and lay them on peoples' shoulders, but they will not lift a finger to move them." (Mt 23:1–2)

Once again Jesus honors the law but not the teachers who preach but do not practice it. He goes on to contrast the public behavior of such teachers who seek recognition, esteem, or self-gratification based on what their own followers are to do and not do. And then he directs a series of seven "Woes" toward the scribes and the Pharisees, each more descriptive, devastating, and damning that the one before. He condemns how they keep people from the kingdom of heaven while not entering it themselves, and decries their inner filth and the corruption of their religious practices. He reviles their careful attention to legalistic details, at the expense of the human person in front of them, which is the measure of true worship and obedience to the covenant. He ends by describing them as white-washed tombs and descendents of those who murdered the prophets. Jesus speaks with the rage of a prophet who upholds God's honor, who condemns the absence of justice while these scribes and Pharisees continue with empty ritual that to God is not worship, but an insult. This chapter of woes, of denunciations and accusations, ends with Jesus lamenting over Jerusalem, the city, the nation, and the people:

> Jerusalem, Jerusalem, you who kill the prophets and stone those sent to you, how many times I yearned to gather your children together, as a hen gathers her young under her wings, but you were unwilling. Behold, your house will be abandoned, desolate. I tell you, you will not see me again until you say, "Blessed is he who comes in the name of the Lord." (Mt 23:37–39)

Even though Jesus rails against those who have betrayed the people's trust, his words reveal his love for the law and covenant and his desire that his own people know God, the Father he sought to share with them. He reiterates that he will die in Jerusalem, as did the prophets who preceded him. He too, "from the righteous blood of Abel to the blood of Zechariah, the son of Barachiah, who was murdered between the sanctuary and the altar" (Mt 23:35) will die, completing the litany of the martyred with his own person.

In chapter 24, using apocalyptic language, imagery, and symbols from the prophets, especially Daniel, Jesus speaks of the destruction of the temple and the persecutions, trials, and tribulations to come. He is not telling the future but speaking of present realities, pronouncing judgment from God's point of view upon the nations of the earth. He describes the coming in glory of the Son of Man, a term that he has used to describe himself in foretelling his crucifixion and death, and in lessons and parables that deal with justice and judgment. The chapter concludes with the story of a wicked servant who does not heed the hour of his master's return:

> Immediately after the tribulation of those days, the sun will be darkened, and the moon will not give its light, and the stars will fall from the sky, and the powers of the heavens will be shaken. And then the sign of the Son of Man will appear in heaven, and all the tribes of the earth will mourn, and they will see the Son of Man coming upon the clouds of heaven with power and great glory. And he will send out his angels with a trumpet blast, and they will gather his elect from the four winds, from one end of the heavens to the other. (Mt 24:29–31)

Who is this Son of Man? In the book of Daniel, chapter 8, he appears as one who comes in glory, drawing all of heaven and earth together. He is one who comes to judge the nations with justice, one who comes as a human being who has suffered much at the hands of people and so bears the right to judge with justice. The image of the Son of Man carries the same symbolic significance as the Lamb of God in the book of Exodus, its blood smeared on the doorposts of those to be liberated from Pharaoh's slavery. It is also connected closely with the Good Shepherd who gathers and tends his sheep, the one who, having separated them from the goats, will sit in judgment over the nations of the world, declaring justice and mercy for the least as the mark of those who are saved and who will dwell in the kingdom of heaven forever. Because Jesus refers to himself as the Son of Man always in the context of being rejected, handed over to torture, to be beaten, mocked, scourged, and crucified, this human being is the suffering servant of Yahweh who obeys God, honors God and speaks truthfully of God in the face of opposition, hatred, even his own murder. Daniel sees him as one coming with light and glory to vindicate the just and the poor. The story of the transfiguration, when Peter, James, and John catch a glimpse of Jesus' soul, echoes all the elements of the description of the Son of Man. The Son of Man is the crucified and risen Jesus, beloved servant and son of the Father, coming in the glory and power of the Spirit to judge all the nations because he alone, in his own body, in his own suffering and death, can judge with justice and with mercy. This is the Son of Man. This is who Jesus believes himself to be in all of the gospels. He faces the city of Jerusalem and the temple that will fall because of Israel's collusion with the Romans and the divisions among its people, and he, God with us, God's own child, declares himself The Prophet of God, the Word of God and the Son of Man.

In his account of the passion and death of Jesus, Matthew reveals the collusion between one of Jesus' own and the leaders of the people. For thirty pieces of silver, Judas, a willing accomplice in the chief priests' dirty work, hands him over. Their plot unfolds on the Feast of the Unleavened Bread, after the evening meal celebrating Passover — the deliverance of the people. Jesus sits at table with his twelve disciples, part of the inner core of the family-like community gathered around him. Even though he knows what Judas intends to do, Jesus eats with them and drinks the ritual cups of wine. During the meal Jesus even informs them that one of his intimate community would betray him, and then tells Peter in front of the entire group that Peter not will only betray him but will declare he doesn't even know Jesus and will curse his name. Yet Peter still eats with him at this last supper together.

During the Passover ritual, the celebration of deliverance, Jesus focuses on the bread and the cup of wine and speaks of the new covenant of forgiveness. What he has often done on hillsides and in deserted places he now does as his parting gesture, giving his last gift to them — his own body to sustain them on the way of the cross that leads to the Father, in the power of the Spirit.

> While they were eating, Jesus took bread, said the blessing, broke it, and giving it to his disciples said, "Take and eat; this is my body." Then he took a cup, gave thanks, and gave it to them saying, "Drink from it, all of you, for this is my blood of the covenant, which will be shed on behalf of many for the forgiveness of sins. I tell you that I will not drink this fruit of the vine until the day when I drink it with you new in the kingdom of my Father." (Mt 26:26–29)

Once again, Jesus' farewell contains images of vineyards, workers, and the fruit of the vine. Moreover, he tells them that they will all have their faith in him shaken to its core, "… for it is written: 'I will strike the shepherd, and the sheep of the flock will be dispersed' " (Mt 26:31). He goes to the garden on the Mount of Olives to pray and to face what awaits him there. He falls prostrate before his Father, the only time he does so before anyone, and cries out in agony and in obedience. He returns to his dozing, unaware followers, seeking to tell them once again that the Son of Man will be handed over. He has given them and us the food and drink of his kingdom, his body. He has given his words and parables, his example and his prayer. He has sung with them and traveled with them and lived with them and now with them — and with us — he will die.

And now Judas' collusion with evil is fulfilled. At the moment of his betrayal Jesus speaks words that will be etched in the disciples' memories. Speaking to Judas, he says: "Friend, do what you have come for" (Mt 26:50). To the last, even knowing what Judas has done, Jesus calls him friend. With Jesus, we are always friends. And then, even amidst the chaos, hatred, and violence as he is seized, Jesus remains teacher and lord.

Then stepping forward they laid hands on Jesus and arrested him. And behold, one of those who accompanied Jesus put his hand to his sword, drew it, and struck the high priest's servant, cutting off his ear. Then Jesus said to him, "Put your sword back into its sheath, for all who take the sword will perish by the sword. Do you think that I cannot call upon my Father and he will not provide me at this moment with more than twelve legions of angels? But then how would the scriptures be fulfilled which say that it must come to pass in this way?" At that hour, Jesus said to the crowds. "Have you come out as against a robber, with swords and clubs to seize me? Day after day I sat teaching in the temple area, yet you did not arrest me. But all this has come to pass that the writings of the prophets may be fulfilled." Then all the disciples left him and fled. (Mt 26:50b–56)

The passion account must have heartened Jesus' followers when they found themselves walking in his steps, facing betrayal, arrest, torture, and death. His example reveals how to react. His disciples must resist the temptation to test God by presuming that they will be saved, or by using violence. These last words the disciples heard from Jesus we must take to heart today: "Put your sword back into its sheath, for all who take the sword will perish by the sword." Jesus' disciples must love their enemies, bless those who persecute them, forgive them as they die and rely on the power of God to vindicate them in God's time. Facing their own pain, they must imitate Jesus in his sufferings.

After a sham trial before the high priest at which false witnesses twist Jesus' words, the Sanhedrin condemn him to death, but they cannot kill him. Only the detested Roman procurator can do that; to obtain a sentence of death they must make Jesus out to be a traitor to Rome, as dangerous to the empire as he is to the Jewish community. In Matthew's account everything that happens around Jesus is despicable and shameful. Peter's three ever-more-vehement denials sever him from Jesus. Judas hangs himself. The disciples cringe and hide. The leaders play falsely. Pilate asks him if he is the king of the

Jews, but Jesus answers only indirectly, and does not respond at all
when Pilate accuses him, using the words of the trial before the high
priest. Jesus speaks only before the high priest, and his words are a
declaration of faith for Matthew's community. They too face intimi-
dation by the Jewish leaders and, often betrayed by their neighbors,
family, friends, even by those within the community of believers,
they face persecution and martyrdom at the hands of the Romans.
Jesus declares:

> From now on you will see "the Son of Man seated at the
> right hand of the Power" and "coming on the clouds of
> heaven." (Mt 26:64)

This is the child of mercy, the child of God, the forgiveness of
God who reconciles everyone to the Father and who gathers all the
peoples into the Spirit making us one in God. For this, he dies. And
many of those who believe and put their trust in Jesus and our Father
and the Spirit will also die. At his trial, no one speaks the truth. No
one testifies to what Jesus has done and said. No one stands up
for Jesus. The ugly process commences: a sentence of death, a
scourging by the Roman soldiers to reduce the convict to the edge of
death, and the laying of the beam across the prisoner's shoulders, as
all slaves bore the yoke of their masters. During the only moment of
compassion Simon of Cyrene takes the burden from Jesus' shoulders so that Jesus can make it to the place of execution. It is the only
grace-filled touch on the way of the cross. Jesus is crucified, mocked
by his own people, and left to die between two terrorists who sought
to overthrow the Roman government in Palestine. Even they join in
reviling him, sneering "He trusted in God," but that indeed was the
truth. After refusing the wine-soaked sponge, Jesus cries out, "My
God, my God, why have you forsaken me?" and gives up his spirit
(Mt 27:56). It is done. It is over. Then havoc follows in the city and
the temple, and the Roman soldiers who executed him declare:
"Truly, this was the Son of God!" (Mt 27:54).

As we do after the ritual remembrance on Good Friday it is best that we remain silent, to take all this to heart, to hold it within us and to share our grief with others, to go home to the darkness and the long night of sorrow asking ourselves whether we pick up the cross in our lives, whether we bear one another's burdens, as did Simon, the man of Cyrene.

Questions:

1. Jesus accuses the leaders of his own religion of hypocrisy. Unfortunately, human nature, even among Jesus' own followers, does not change. Aware of your own human weakness, what behavior or practices in church leadership today do you see need special scrutiny? Who do such behavior or practices affect the most?

2. Jesus' seven statements that begin "Woe to you ..." are like an examination of conscience for those who exercise leadership or authority at any level of the church. Which of the seven suggests how a group you belong to might claim to be serving the people of God, but in reality is scandalizing them?

3. Everyone betrays Jesus. No one stands up for him and says what Jesus has done for them. Who in the passion account mirrors the shortcomings in your own relationship with Jesus: Peter; Judas; the other disciples; the leaders and elders of the community; the high priest; those crucified with him; the soldiers who are just doing their job, but who actually scourge, humiliate, and insult him; the mob that lets itself be led by its religious and civic leaders?

4. Jesus is handed over to be killed, yet he hands over his spirit to God. Sit and pray, with Jesus handing over your spirit to God, trying to put into words what you would say with your last breath.

10

"I Am with You All Days,
Even to the End of Time"

In Matthew's account of Jesus' death, Jesus screams twice before dying, a common occurrence among those being crucified. In first-hand accounts of crucifixions what people described most were the screams that shattered their ears, their minds, and their hearts, sticking in their memories. They were screams of rage, hopelessness, prayer, entreaty, frustration, pure pain and despair. The words Jesus screams are lines from the psalms, the prayer of someone trusting in God as he hung in agony and a scream of pain and handing over to God his spirit, his body and soul and his heart. And then all hell breaks loose: an earthquake rocks the city, splitting and shattering boulders, tearing the veil of the temple in two and opening the graves of the righteous, who enter the city and serve as messengers. The tearing of the veil of the temple is the most significant for it symbolizes that at Jesus' death nothing any longer separates us from the presence of God. There is no barrier, no gulf, no chasm. We now stand before God, with Jesus, in the power of the Holy Spirit. Our God is with us, close, near.

And then Matthew recounts more mundane aspects: removing the body of Jesus from the cross, making preparations for burying him, and ensuring that they had finished what they could do before the Sabbath. But in Matthew's account of the passion, death, and resurrection of Jesus these details are important. They follow a distinct motif, beginning with the women disciples and Joseph of Arimathea, moving to the Pharisees and priests, then to the solders standing guard at the tomb. The pattern of what happens at the resurrection will repeat the motif: after the resurrection the women leave the empty tomb to tell the other disciples; the soldiers tell the Jewish leaders, who continue to collude with the Romans and to conspire together, refusing to entertain any other explanation for the empty tomb. Then there is the last story of Jesus, once again with his disciples on a mountain. Matthew began his story with the horror and slaughter that accompanied the birth of this child named Emmanuel and he ends it with the violence of the crucifixion and the repeated betrayal and collusion, in which religious leaders bow to political and military power. This reality that Matthew's church faced still lives on. All members of Jesus' church, leaders and flock alike, must remember Jesus' admonitions not to imitate the actions of others, but to imitate only him.

Matthew's Gospel does not contain an account of the resurrection. It explains what precedes that mystery and what has happened since, even its impact on all of history — all empires, all nations, all time, even every individual. The resurrection is like the epicenter of an earthquake from which shocks emanate outward in larger and larger circles, shaking every foundation. Two mysteries — the Incarnation and the Resurrection — undergird our faith and our life as those who bear the wisdom and the light of Jesus, the Christ, Emmanuel, God with us. Matthew states three obvious facts: Jesus died. He was buried in the tomb. The tomb is empty. Each group of people who become aware of these facts tell a different story about how the tomb became empty, where the body of Jesus is, and what it means for humankind. We too must face these facts. There is a story that perhaps can make us pause and ask ourselves what we think happened to Jesus' body and what it means that the tomb is empty. Perhaps this story can help us start wondering, praying, reflecting, and realizing that it is a mystery to be probed, but ultimately a mystery to dwell in:

> * Ludwig von Beethoven had been working on a new sonata for weeks. Finally he sat down at the piano to play it for a group of friends and curious onlookers. He poured himself into it, oblivious to everything but the notes that cascaded and swirled around him and out to those who were listening. When he

finished he let out a deep sigh of release and relief. Slowly he turned toward his audience. Abruptly one person said: "Yes, but what does the music mean?" Beethoven was not pleased. He scowled at the man furiously and turned back to the keyboard and replayed the entire sonata with the same passion, grace, and intensity. He finished, turned to his questioner, and with a great smile said: "That is what it means!"

No matter what we say about the resurrection, about the body of Jesus, crucified and risen from the dead, we must start from the moment of knowing nothing and seeking to believe so that we might come to some insight and understanding. We must stake our lives on its reality and let its power inform the way we dig into the inspired scriptures so that we can live the resurrection into which we are initiated at our baptisms. Somehow Jesus' resurrection life is our own baptismal life and all our lives we are to grow in its wisdom, its power and grace. In living through it we learn to be able to speak about it.

Matthew connects three groups of people with Jesus' death and burial as well as with the empty tomb and what follows. After Jesus dies, Matthew describes what the women do. The men disciples in Matthew's Gospel are more problematic, with weaknesses in their belief and in their willingness to follow Jesus or to practice what he teaches. But the women disciples, often unnamed (like Peter's mother-in-law, the Canaanite woman, the woman who touches the hem of his garment and the last woman he encounters before the Passover, in Simon the leper's house, who anoints him in public) reveal an immediate understanding and acceptance of Jesus. The men question or hesitate, but the women act upon their hopes. Matthew notes that they are the witnesses to Jesus' death:

> There were many women there, looking on from a distance, who had followed Jesus from Galilee, ministering to him. Among them were Mary Magdalene and Mary the mother of James and Joseph, and the mother of the sons of Zebedee. (Mt 27:55–56)

He names three: Mary of Magdala, named first in the resurrection accounts of all four gospels, suggesting her status as a leader and disciple known to the entire church community; Mary the mother of James and Joseph, about whom nothing else is mentioned; and the mother of Zebedee's sons, James and John. She is the one who asked Jesus that her sons be seated in his kingdom on either side of his throne. All of the women called Mary (in Hebrew, Myriam) are named after the sister of Moses, who saved him from death as a child so that he could grow up to be the liberator and law giver of Israel. Jesus, the new liberator and law giver to all the world, is surrounded by Myriams who have "ministered" to him. The word "ministered," the same as in the account of the temptations when the angels came and ministered to Jesus, denotes public service in the community. Now, at a public execution, they watch helplessly from a distance. The only men allowed near a crucifixion were the executioners, but these women can witness the death of Jesus. They will figure strongly in what follows.

Next, Matthew mentions another Joseph. The gospel begins and ends with men named Joseph — the first gives his life daily to save the life of Jesus, the Beloved child of God, so that he will grow to be a man. Now there is another Joseph who follows, but like the women he has up until now been silent, unacknowledged, or had done nothing in public to align himself with Jesus. But the fact that he is named means that he, too, is a disciple and a part of Matthew's church:

> When it was evening, there came a rich man from Arimathea named Joseph, who was himself a disciple of Jesus. He went to Pilate and asked for the body of Jesus; then Pilate ordered it to be handed over. Taking the body, Joseph wrapped it (in) clean linen and laid it in his new tomb that he had hewn in the rock. Then he rolled a huge stone across the entrance to the tomb and departed. But Mary Magdalene and the other Mary remained sitting there, facing the tomb. (Mt 27:57–61)

The death of Jesus has propelled Joseph into risking his life and all he owns by claiming the body of Jesus and burying it in his own tomb, actions which suggest that he may be an elderly man anticipating his own death. He wraps the body in linen as the first Joseph wrapped the newborn child in swaddling clothes and laid him in a manger. Now the human child is buried, as are all human beings after death. He rolls a great stone in front of the entrance to keep others out. But the women who have followed the body to Joseph's burial place keep watch. They hold vigil facing the tomb, as they most probably often sat at Jesus' feet, watching him and listening to his words. They stay until night falls and they must go to honor the Sabbath.

Then the next group of people to appear are conspirators — the Jewish and the Roman authorities. Concerned even about the dead body of Jesus, they feel the need to make sure it stays in the tomb. They display the same fear, insecurity, and cold-blooded calculation in their response after Jesus' death that they showed as they sought it so earnestly:

> The next day, the one following the day of preparation, the chief priests and the Pharisees gathered before Pilate and said, "Sir, we remember that this imposter while still alive said, 'After three days I will be raised up.' Give orders, then, that the grave be secured until the third day, lest his disciples come and steal him and say to the people, 'He has been raised from the dead.' This last imposture would be worse than the first." Pilate said to them, "The guard is yours; go secure it as best you can." So they went and secured the tomb by fixing a seal to the stone and setting the guard. (Mt 27:62–66)

They are trying to foresee any circumstances that could make the situation even worse: a prophet in Israel tortured and murdered by the Romans at the behest of the Jewish leadership. And if those who are willing to stake their lives on the reality of an empty tomb and the resurrection claim that it happened, the Jewish leaders can claim that such believers have concocted a conspiracy of lies. Pilate authorizes sending a contingent to guard a dead body and placing an official seal on the tomb, making it a crime to break it. The chief priests and Pharisees make their request on the day "following the day of preparation," which would be the Sabbath; such activity would certainly violate Jewish law. And even though Pilate wields the military might of

Rome, his words reveal insecurity: "… go secure it as best you can." Matthew is making sure that believers see the futility of the power of the empire before the power of Jesus' words and his life.

After the Sabbath the women appear again, going to visit the tomb. They have obeyed the law of rest and now continue their grieving by returning to the tomb. When they arrive just after dawn, the resurrection itself has already happened. Matthew shrouds it in mystery. No one witnesses God the Father raising Jesus from the dead in the power and love of the Spirit. Once again everything in creation breaks loose with another earthquake, this time an angel descending from heaven, rolling away the stone, and sitting on it. The angel is compared to lightning, clothed in blinding light like sun on snow. Matthew contrasts the reactions of the women and the guards:

> The guards were shaken with fear of him and became like dead men. Then the angel said to the women in reply, "Do not be afraid! I know that you are seeking Jesus the crucified. He is not here, for he has been raised just as he said. Come and see the place where he lay. Then go quickly and tell his disciples, 'He has been raised from the dead, and he is going before you to Galilee; there you will see him.' Behold I have told you." Then they went away quickly from the tomb, fearful yet overjoyed, and ran to announce this to his disciples. (Mt 28:4–8)

Both groups are filled with fear. The soldiers collapse as if dead, but the women stand their ground, even if quaking. The initial words of the resurrection proclamation, which echo what Jesus often said to his followers, go straight to their hearts: "Do not be afraid!" This statement, which Matthew's community took as a proclamation of belief, is announced by an angel, just as news of the birth of Jesus came to Joseph. Angels appear at the beginning and at the end of the story. The community of Matthew seeks Jesus the crucified, the Son of Man, and he is risen from the dead. They will not find him in a tomb. They must go home and seek him there in their lives where they first met him, heard the words of repentance, and learned of the presence of the kingdom of heaven come to earth in his person. The women are invited into the tomb to see the place of burial and then are sent forth to announce the resurrection, specifically to bring the good news to the other disciples. Since the very beginnings of the church, to enter the tomb has meant to enter the waters of baptism and to rise to resurrection life, emboldened by the Spirit and gifted with the wisdom and knowledge that seeks to be proclaimed and shared. It is the two Marys who first enter the tomb, emerge baptized by the Spirit, and are sent to proclaim the gospel. They obey immediately, as did Joseph at the beginning of the gospel, and their obedience is rewarded with the actual presence of Jesus, their crucified and risen Lord:

> Then they went away quickly from the tomb, fearful yet overjoyed, and ran to announce this to his disciples. And behold, Jesus met them on their way and greeted them. They approached, embraced his feet, and did him homage. Then Jesus said to them, "Do not be afraid. Go tell my brothers to go to Galilee, and there they will see me." (Mt 28:10)

Keyed up with fear and joy, they run. With Jesus they walk but with resurrection's strength they can run! When Jesus greets them, we can imagine that he must have used the words that Luke and John have him speak after the resurrection, "Peace be with you!" As did those who sought his power, such as the Magi, the centurion seeking a cure for his servant, and the Canaanite woman pleading that Jesus help her troubled daughter, they do him homage and worship him. Jesus commissions them, sending them to summon the other disciples to Galilee, where he will meet them. With one word, Jesus forgives the disciples' absence, betrayal, fear, lack of faith, and failure to walk with him to the cross in Jerusalem. He calls them "brothers." The relationship with his Father, our Father, that he has shared with them, the same that binds us together as his brothers and sisters in the love of the Spirit, still holds. Not even death can break it. There is no reason to fear — anyone, anything, ever. The presence of the risen Lord is with us.

Matthew then turns to the soldiers heading into Jerusalem to explain to the chief priests what happened. Because they had been hired, they will have to explain their failure to guard the tomb — to those who had paid them and to their own military commanders. The pattern of conspiracy holds until the end. The chief priests and the elders give the soldiers a large sum of money and tell them what to say, with the assurance that they will cover for them with Pilate. Matthew then sums up the growing split between the Christian communities and the Jewish leadership: "And this story has circulated among the Jews to the present (day)" (Mt 28:15).

The startlingly new final paragraph reveals how the church has grown since the middle sixties when Mark's earlier gospel was probably written. About twenty five years have passed and the power of the Spirit that gives word, wisdom, witness, and power to believers has been at work, moving out into every area of the empire and beyond. Matthew describes what is already happening in the churches, once again reminding them of who Jesus is, who they follow, and what they are to do in obedience to his words, life, death, and resurrection. The disciples and all those who traveled together to Jerusalem for the Passover earlier that week would have returned over ninety miles of rough road to Galilee, a place referred to as "Galilee of the Gentiles" (see Is 8:23, Mt 4:15), for this is Matthew's community — the whole world that lies beyond the horizon of time and space. About ten days to two weeks later they would have gathered on a mountain — the mountain of the Beatitudes, the mountain of the Transfiguration, or one of the places where Jesus fed the people — and from this mountain God's Word will go forth. The women have provided the link between the world of the soldiers, the realm of death and burial, and the mountaintop from which the power of heaven will extend into the world. The disciples have been trying to avoid realities that from the beginning Jesus has wanted them to face. Now they will see:

> The eleven disciples went to Galilee, to the mountain to which Jesus had ordered them. When they saw him, they worshiped, but they doubted. Then Jesus approached and said to them, "All power in heaven and on earth has been given to me. Go, therefore, and make disciples of all nations, baptizing them in the name of the Father, and of the Son, and of the Holy Spirit, teaching them to observe all that I have commanded you. And behold, I am with you always, until the end of the age." (Mt 28:16–20)

Matthew mentions the eleven, but many others must have also been there, such as the women and others, like Joseph of Arimathea, who had been with Jesus since the beginning of his preaching in Galilee. As they have done throughout the gospel, they all go to the mountain together to listen to the Word of God in Jesus, now the risen Lord. But Matthew focuses on the eleven because they did not see him die or watch him be buried. They must see him now. They do, but — as Matthew notes — "some doubted." This was the disturbing truth in Matthew's communities, and in our own churches today it still is. Some, even leaders within the community, doubt. Like Jesus, Matthew does not shy away from telling his community the truth. Then as now, it is Jesus himself who approaches to share his presence, the Word, the revelation of God and the power of his Spirit.

He begins by assuring them that all power in heaven and on earth has been given to him — all power. A motif of power has run through the entire Gospel of Matthew. In the story of the Magi, we have seen how power that was supposed to bring hope to all people was subverted by the ruthless and murderous Herod and used to destroy possibility and life. We have heard Satan offer the powers of the earth — nations, money, fear, insecurity, might, collusion among enemies, law and institutional structures bent on solidification and extension of their own power — if Jesus will do him homage. We have seen the power of law without compassion, worship without sacrifice, judgment without mercy, and fear that paralyzes, mutes, and makes deaf. We have seen the power of mobs, molded into screaming masses bent on destruction that denies, isolates, excludes, and ultimately destroys the very humanity of other human beings. We have seen the power of Rome: governor, soldiers, executioners, guards, occupation, enslavement, taxes, money minted with the image of a man who claims to be a god. All of these, though they still stand in opposition to God's presence on earth, are powerless against the power of God in Jesus.

Jesus' power is the power of heaven: the power of the Spirit of God; the power of forgiveness, reconciliation, at-one-ment, mercy, and love. Jesus' power is the power of the Trinity; the power of initiation into the Trinity, into the family of the beloved children of God, the brothers and sisters of Jesus, especially those who are the least, the poorest, the most powerless, the neediest. Jesus' power is the power of listening to and obeying the Word of the Beatitudes, blessing and hope, the Good News of God. Jesus' power is the power of love, love unto death, love without harm, love without violence, love without discrimination, love without limits, love that even death cannot stop. It is love best expressed in ritual, in sacrament, in community, in teaching by example, and in sustained hope. It is the power of Emmanuel, God with us.

And Jesus gives this power to use as he did, in trust for others. The eleven, all the other disciples, and the church are pushed outside their usual borders, boundaries, and limits, beyond their traditions, fears, insecurities, and past, out past the horizon into every nation and every place on earth. He tells them to do three things, in this order:

1. To make disciples from every nation. The church is to be gathered from every place on the face of the earth. The faithful are to be drawn into a community by seeing, watching, hearing, practicing what believers do. They are to be gathered through the witness of community living and unity, communion among the members. This comes first so those who wish to belong know what they are being drawn into — the Trinity of God and God's community that mirrors those relationships here on earth.

2. After gathering those who wish to follow the way of the cross, the way of Jesus to the Father, the way of the Spirit in the law, to baptize them. They are to be baptized in the name of the Trinity: Father, Son, and Spirit. When Matthew writes this, it is already the practice of the community, the ritual that initiates persons into the Trinity. Jesus, in the power of the Spirit, makes them beloved children of God, brothers or sisters to all others. Then they dwell in the Trinity, with the community of the Body of Christ, immersed in the power of the Spirit.

3. To teach the baptized to observe all that Jesus has commanded them. Today this happens during the mystogogia, the
time of instruction during which baptized adults are drawn
deeper and deeper into the mysteries they now experience
together with the Body of Christ. And the mystogogia
continues. Just as the creation recounted in Genesis has
begun, is ongoing, and will be until the end of time, the
church is created in the same pattern: making disciples,
baptizing in the name of the Trinity, and teaching by
observing, obeying, imitating, and practicing all of the
law and the teachings of Jesus. Observation, obedience,
the practice of virtue, forgiving, reconciling, healing,
feeding, including, atoning, restoring, repairing, uniting,
freeing, communing, praying — this is being church. This
is being and becoming community. This is witnessing to
the presence of God with us in the risen Lord.

Jesus abides with us always, all ways. His last word is, "I am with
you always." He is with us in presence, power, and person. Yet these
words mean more. He is the Word spoken out loud: "I Am with you
always." Emmanuel, God-with-us, the name given him by the scriptures and the angel in the beginning is realized in ways that cannot be
comprehended, but must be believed in and embraced, surrendered to
and lived, not as individuals but together with others in community.
Jesus is God, the God of creation and Genesis; the God of patriarchs
and matriarchs, the God of Moses and the law, the God of the prophets,
the God of the Exodus and the exile, the God of the promises and
hopes, the God of the earlier covenant and testament, the God of the
living, the God of Israel. And Jesus is the God revealed in the mysteries
of the Incarnation, the Resurrection, the Body of Christ that is Word,
Eucharist and Community, and the Trinity. Jesus is the God of justice
and mercy, of forgiveness and reconciliation, and the one who in the
Trinity makes us all one in God. This is the beginning of our belief.
This is the genesis of the communities of Church. This is the origin of
the kingdom of heaven on earth, entrusted to us. This is how Matthew
tries to bring some closure to a story without end and tries to catapult

his community, as fearful and insecure, doubting and betraying as those who first followed Jesus into the world that waits and watches for them and hungers for the good news in Jesus, the Son of Man, beloved of God, servant, prophet, healer, law giver, liberator, teacher, reconciler, shepherd, judge, our brother, and the fullness of the Spirit of justice, peace, and mercy. This is not the end. This is Matthew's way, seventy to one hundred years after the life, death, and resurrection of Jesus, of beginning. It begins now, here, among us, our God with us. The power is shared with us. What are we doing with it? We dwell in the Trinity, in the kingdom of heaven on earth. God is not completely delighted with us until all are one in the Trinity and all are invited into this mystery of intimacy and presence. Those who have ears to hear, Listen! Those who have eyes to see, Look! Those who seek the crucified and risen Jesus: Hand over your lives to God and pray in the Spirit of Jesus, with Jesus:

> I give praise to you, Father, Lord of heaven and earth, for although you have hidden these things from the wise and the learned you have revealed them to the childlike. Yes, Father, such has been your gracious will. All things have been handed over to me by my Father. No one knows the Son except the Father, and no one knows the Father except the Son and anyone to whom the Son wishes to reveal him. (Mt 11:25–27)

There must be a story with which to end — or from which to begin. Matthew's Gospel is about power, and the power of God is the Spirit of God, the presence of the risen Jesus among us. This is what has been shared and given to us so that we might be the light, the truth, and the glorious forgiveness and mercy of God in the world. The story with which I will conclude is also a story about the Spirit, the power entrusted to us, a jumping-off place, a place for a vision that sets us facing the world. It comes from an account by Laurens van der Post.[1] This story was told by the groups of bushmen with whom he traveled

---

1. "The Wilderness Within," *Utne Reader,* February/March 1985, 122–126.

and observed. Each group numbered just twenty-three individuals, each of whom was essential to the survival of the community. Every group told this same one of their core stories:

* Once upon a time there was a great hunter. He had been blessed with the gift of hunting food so that no one in the village would ever go hungry. As it often was, this man was also blessed with the gift of music. He was as skillful with the bow he used in hunting as he was with bow on his musical instrument. Both his gifts fed his people. Well, one day while hunting he stopped to drink from a pool. It was the rainy season and there was an abundance of water. He drank and as he finished he saw reflected in the water, against the bright blue African sky, a bird, a great white bird, unlike any he had ever seen before. It was a momentary flash that seared his mind and soul. He looked up quickly but the bird was gone.

He returned to the village utterly changed. He lost all interest in hunting and had to be persuaded to make music. He abandoned any thought of killing, even to feed others. He was not distraught or unhappy; but he lived hungry, yearning and wanting desperately to see that great white bird again. The people were distressed. They loved him but they needed his skills and gifts. Finally he bent before them and told them he was leaving. He was deeply sorrowful, but he just could not live as he did before. He had to leave and find the great white bird that for just a fleeting moment had hovered over him. He left and in his village was never seen again.

They say that he traveled all over Africa, telling people about the great white bird and asking them if they had ever seen it or knew where he could find it. Many had seen it, and they would tell him what they knew about the bird and if it came more than once. He never again caught sight of it. He lived on the word of anyone who had seen it, taking it to heart and moving on, knowing he had to see it again before he died. Life was hard on the road. He grew old, and one day he knew that it was soon to be the time of his dying. He found himself in a village at the foot of a mountain and once again he asked about the bird. The people not only knew of the bird, on the mountain above them it nested! Though exhausted, the man was overjoyed. Immediately, his strength failing, he began to climb, slowing with each step and breath. How he longed to see the bird again. He looked in every crack in the stone, on every crag and from every point overlooking the valley, searching for the nest or even a glimpse of the bird returning to feed its young or sailing on the wind currents. The sun was setting in fire and dying light against the blue-black of oncoming night. He looked up and saw a great white feather drifting down toward him on the soft dying evening breeze. He did not see the bird, but he caught the silky feather in his hand, marveling at it. As he grasped it, his spirit left him. He died.

Van der Post says that when the bushmen told him this story, he asked them: "What sort of bird was it?" And they answered: "The bird has many names, but we think of it as the Great White Bird of Truth." We have been given of this Spirit, this Truth, this Power of God and we must seek to know ever more deeply the wisdom of God in Jesus who was filled so completely with the Spirit. We must stretch out our hands, reach with our minds and hearts and together make the dream of God, the truth of God come true today, in our world, on earth. The resurrection of Jesus, the presence of God among us, is a gift of life, a gift of resurgence, a gift that sends us off into the world to share what has been given to us. As the women who left the tomb, obeying Jesus' words, in the peace of the risen Lord, we too "Go in peace, to love and serve the Lord, in one another and in the world."

Questions

1. To which group do you find yourself belonging: the anonymous or little-mentioned disciples such as the women or Joseph of Arimethea; the public leadership of the church, both men and women; the religious authorities who collude

with local or national government officials; or soldiers in the hire of others?

2. Do you doubt? What? How do you express your doubt? Doubt means that you know what is proclaimed but do not put it into practice because of its cost, because you would have to change, or because you cannot make rational sense of it. In any case you do not obey because of your weakness, your failure to believe, or your reluctance to trust in God.

3. Are you a disciple of Jesus, the crucified and risen Lord of heaven and earth, or merely one who claims to believe in Jesus? What are some of the characteristics that distinguish disciples from believers?

4. Do you pray to the Trinity? Do you dwell in the Trinity? Do you practice communion and unity in the Trinity with others? Share with each other how you practice these basic elements of your faith.

Works Cited

Chacour, Elias, and Mary Evelyn Jensen. *We Belong to the Land.* San Francisco: Harper, 1990.

Davenport, Gene. *Into the Darkness: Discipleship and the Sermon on the Mount.* Nashville: Abingdon Press, 1988.

Merton, Thomas. "Blessed Are the Meek: The Roots of Christian Nonviolence." *Fellowship Magazine*, May 1967, 18–22.

Ter Linden, Nico. *The Story Goes ... Mark's Story and Matthew's Story.* London: SCM Press, 1999.

For Further Reading

Books on Matthew and Scripture

Albright, W. F. and C. S. Mann. *Matthew (Anchor Bible), A New Translation with Introduction and Commentary.* New York, NY: Doubleday, 1971.

Aune, David E. *The Gospel of Matthew in Current Study.* Grand Rapids, MI: William Eerdmans Publishing Company, 2001.

Brown, Raymond E. *The Birth of the Messiah: A Commentary on the Infancy Narratives in Matthew and Luke.* Garden City, NY: Doubleday and Co., Inc., 1977.

Buckley, Thomas W. *Seventy Times Seven: Sin, Judgment, and Forgiveness in Matthew,* Zacchaeus Studies NT, Collegeville, MN: Liturgical Press, 1991.

Byrne, Brendan: *Lifting the Burden: Reading Matthew's Gospel in the Church Today.* Collegeville, MN: Liturgical Press, 2004.

Carter, Warren. *Matthew and Empire: Initial Explorations.* Harrisburg, PA: Trinity Press International, 2001.

_____. *Matthew and the Margins: A Sociopolitical and Religious Reading.* Maryknoll, NY: Orbis Books, 2000.

Crosby, Michael. *House of Disciples: Church, Economics, and Justice in Matthew.* Maryknoll, NY: Orbis Books, 1988.

_____. *Spirituality of the Beatitudes: Matthew's Vision for the Church in an Unjust World.* Maryknoll, NY: Orbis Books, 2005.

_____. *Thy Will Be Done: Praying the Our Father as Subversive Activity.* Maryknoll, NY: Orbis Books, 1977.

Echegaray, Hugo. *The Practice of Jesus.* Maryknoll, NY: Orbis Books, 1984.

Ellis, Peter F. *Matthew: His Mind and His Message.* Collegeville, MN: Liturgical Press, 1974.

Hanson, K.C. and Douglas Oakman. *Palestine in the Time of Jesus: Social Structures and Social Conflicts.* Minneapolis, MN: Fortress Press, 1998.

Harrington, Wilfried J. *Matthew: Sage Theologian: The Jesus of Matthew.* Dublin, Ireland: The Columba Press, 1998.

Hendrickx, Herman. *A Key to the Gospel of Matthew.* Quezon City, Philippines: Claretian Publications, 1992.

_____. *The Household of God.* Quezon City, Philippines: Claretian Publications, 1992.

Hoppe, Leslie J. *A Retreat with Matthew: Going Beyond the Law.* Cincinnati, OH: St. Anthony Messenger Press, 2000.

Kaylor, David R. *Jesus the Prophet: His Vision of the Kingdom on Earth.* Louisville, KY: Westminster/John Knox Press, 1994.

Kingsbury, Jack D. *Interpretation: The Gospel of Matthew,* A Journal of Bible and Theology 46, #4. Richmond, VA: Union Theological Seminary in Virginia, 1992.

Meier, John P. *Matthew.* New Testament Message 3. Collegeville, MN: Liturgical Press, 1980.

Miller, Ron. *The Hidden Gospel of Matthew: Annotated & Explained.* Woodstock, VT: SkyLight Illuminations, 2004.

Nau, Arlo J. *Peter in Matthew: Discipleship, Diplomacy and Dispraise.* Collegeville, MN: Liturgical Press, 1992.

Perlewitz, Miriam. *The Gospel of Matthew,* Message of Biblical Spirituality #8. Wilmington, DE: Michael Glazier, 1988.

Saint John of Kronstadt. *Ten Homilies on the Beatitudes.* Albany, NY: Cornerstone Editons, La Pierre Angulaire, 2003.

Senior, Donald. *Matthew,* Abingdon New Testament Commentaries. Nashville, TN: Abingdon Press, 1998.

_____. *What Are They Saying about Matthew?* Mahwah, NJ: Paulist Press, 1996.

Stock, Augustine. *The Method and Message of Matthew.* Collegeville, MN: Liturgical Press, 1994.

Trainor, Michael. *A Gospel for Searching People,* Scripture Study Series. Ottawa, Canada: Novalis, 1994.

Wainwright, Elaine M. *Shall We Look for Another? A Feminist Rereading of the Matthean Jesus.* Maryknoll, NY: Orbis Books, 1998.

Preaching Background, Matthew, Cycle A

Bergant, Dianne and Richard Fragomeni. *Preaching the New Lectionary, Year A.* Collegeville, MN: Liturgical Press, 2001.

Eddy, Corbin. *Who Knows the Reach of God? Homilies and Reflections for Year A.* Ottawa, Canada: Novalis, St. Paul University, 2001.

Gutierrez, Gustavo. *Sharing the Word through the Liturgical Year.* Maryknoll, NY: Orbis Books, 1997.

Harrington, Wilfried J. *The Gracious Word: Commentary on Sunday and Holy Day Readings, Year A.* Dublin, Ireland: Dominican Publications, 1995.

McArdle, Jack. *And That's the Gospel Truth: Reflections on the Sunday Gospels, Year A.* Dublin, Ireland: The Columba Press, 2001.

McBride, Alfred. *Year of the Lord, Cycle A.* Dubuque, IA: Wm. C. Brown Publishers, 1983.

McBride, Denis. *Seasons of the World: Reflections on the Sunday Readings.* England: Redemptorist Publications, 1991.

McCarthy, Flor. *New Sunday and Holy Day Liturgies, Year A.* Dublin, Ireland: Dominican Publications and New York, NY: Costello Publishing, 1998. Available for all three cycles.

Pilch, John J. *The Cultural World of Jesus, Sunday by Sunday, Cycle A.* Collegeville, MN: Liturgical Press, 1995.

Race, Marianne and Laurie Brink. *In This Place: Reflections on the Land of the Gospels for the Liturgical Cycles.* Collegeville, MN: Liturgical Press, 1998.

Rotelle, John. *Meditations on the Sunday Gospels, Year A.* Hyde Park, NY: New City Press, 1995.

Shea, John. *Matthew Year A, On Earth As It Is in Heaven: The Spiritual Wisdom of the Gospels for Christian Preachers and Teachers.* Collegeville, MN: Liturgical Press, 2004.

Tubbs Tisdale, Leonora. *The Abingdon Women's Preaching Annual, Series 2. Year A.* Nashville, TN: Abingdon Press, 2001.

Website Postings/Weekly

Daily Gospel, www.dailygospel.org.

National Catholic Reporter, "The Peace Pulpit," Bishop Thomas J. Gumbleton, www.NCRonline.org.

Preaching The Word, Sojourners www.sojo.net.

Sunday by Sunday, Sisters of St. Joseph of Carondelet, 1884 Randolph Ave., St. Paul, MN 55105-1747 (by subscription).

The Word, America Magazine.

Torch Preaching by members of the English Province of the Order of Preachers http://torch.op.org/preaching/sermon.